A CLIMB THROUGH THE MIST

PATIENCE, PERSEVERANCE AND PASSION

JASHANDEEP SINGH KANG

Dedicated to my maternal grandfather Belour Singh Brar
and paternal grandfather Swaran Singh Kang.

Contents

Contents

Contents

Testimonial

"Different people write books for different reasons, but when a young man writes one to pour his heart out through his life-consuming experiences, it is clear that the tempering heat of experience and maturity will put him in to the orbit of celebrity authors in times to come. This book is not quite memoir, not quite biography-but a heady mixture of trials and turbulences of a man on a mission to find what he loves. The author has introduced a dose of magical realism through many interesting anecdotes that make the book highly readable as his style is both elegant and lucid. While walking through with the author, readers can relate with his pain, anguish, ecstasy and joys. He invites the reader to explore more and more and leaves many lessons for people of every age group to help them find their passion. Stamp of his sensitive mind and deep insight in human psychology, is evident in every page of this remarkable book. It is a unique and absorbing story brilliantly told by the first-attempt author, but like established authors, he provides enough leverage to the readers to help them enjoy every page of the book. His first-hand experiences, personal anecdotes and some compassionately narrated l events, make the book a quality literary work.This absorbing book should find a pride of place in personal library of anyone who wants to decipher the alchemy of success."

-Col. D.S. Cheema

(Eminent author, motivational speaker)

Foreword

"If you can force your heart and nerve and sinew,
To serve your turn long after they are gone,
And so hold on when there is nothing in you,
Except the Will which says to them: "Hold on!"
- Rudyard Kipling

I
HORN OF THE TRAIN

It was 1ˢᵗ June 2021 and I woke up from my bed with some nervousness. For 10 years, I had been waiting for this day. It was the day I had to appear for the interview of Punjab civil service exam 2020 in Patiala. A process that had started from nearly sixty thousand candidates had now reduced to a contest among just 175 candidates. I knew that it was one of the toughest state civil service exams, when compared with all of the states in India, because not only I was competing for just 16 seats but the interview panel were to include 10 bureaucrats, unlike other states, where hardly 4-5 members are present in the panel.

Further, I had no experience of driving a car on long routes, so my father had requested one of his office juniors to drive me from Chandigarh to Patiala and I also took my mother with me as she had always been my lucky charm. We had to reach there by 8:30 AM but as fate would have it, at about 8:15 AM there was a rail barrier that blocked the main route to P.P.S.C. office. And once the car was stuck, it was impossible to change the route. The train was just not moving for some reason and *once in a while, it was blowing its loud horn. I knew that a few minutes late would not be an issue but my mother was panicking and so was my father (over the phone call). So my dad's office junior (Harwinder ji), suggested me to cross the rail track and hire an auto from the other side. Somehow I agreed. I hugged my mother and I started walking quickly towards the track. While crossing the track, something made me stop and I looked back at my mother and I kept looking at her....*

Horn of the train......

<u>1977 and my mother</u>

"On one morning of 1977, somebody knocked the door of my grandmother's house (village Tarkhanwala, Muktsar Sahib) and told that a dead body was lying near a canal in the nearby village of Udaangah. A day before, my grandfather Belour Singh Brar had gone to a nearby city of Muktsar, to get his car serviced but he never came back. Along with my 3-year-old mother, my grandmother(pregnant) was left alone that night, worrying for him, as it was quite unusual for his not returning. Few people had also informed my mother's grandfather (then residing in Muktsar) that a person was lying dead and that he looked like his son. He came running first to my village home to check if my grandfather was at home but he wasn't there. Then he took my grandmother to the site. The dead man lying there was my grandfather. There was blood all around. His pistol, bullet belt, and other valuables were missing. Nobody knew what had happened! My 3-year-old mother was a lucky charm for him and it was his dream to see her as a P.C.S. officer. He used to carry her to Muktsar quite often, but that day.. He didn't!

Let me take you a little back! Zamindars, as a class, had emerged during the times of Delhi Sultanate and Jagirdari system of land tenure became quite prominent during the

Mughal times. Zamindars and Jagirdars had proliferated under colonial rule as well. This had led to enormous wealth inequalities amongst the masses and therefore land reforms were logically the first step taken by the Nehru government. But even after land reforms, zamindars continued to possess enormous agro lands. And amongst such people, one was my mother's grandfather. My mother, therefore, belonged to a very affluent family and my maternal grandfather was well educated and a teacher in the village. But things were soon going to change.

On 25 June, 1975, President of India Fakhruddin Ali Ahmed proclaimed a state of national emergency. It all started with inflation, rail strikes, Raj Narain case concerning the election of Indira Gandhi, JP movement, and the events that followed. On one hand Centre had acquired enormous powers, on the other, there was a vacuum of governance at the local levels. This vacuum had led to a deteriorating law and order situation and hence the rising crime levels. It was the same environment that had consumed my grandfather.

Everyone in the village was awestruck at his death. My mother's grandfather had some decent political links and therefore police became active soon after. On other hand, my mother's maternal grandfather, a decorated World War II soldier, led dharnas against the administration for failing to arrest the culprits. All these things made the infamous "Belour Singh murder case of 1977". It was a widely talked about incident and after the end of the national emergency, even the local newspapers had covered the case. Time passed and nearly after 7 years the culprits were arrested from Ganganagar (Rajasthan) and they confessed to committing the murder. They had killed him, just because they had eyes on his pistol and my grandfather had identified them as residents of his village (and hence their previous murders could have been exposed). In a nutshell, life had become so cheap in those times!

Soon after, his property was sold by my mother's grandfather, and that too with acute insensitivity towards the family. And a "well off" life was gradually reduced to a life of daily struggle. Dream of my grandfather to see my mother as a PCS officer was lost and she was married off at the young age of 16 to my father"

And there I stood near the rail track, going for my P.C.S. interview and the noise of that train suddenly stopped. I walked back to my mother and I took her with me. We both somehow crossed the rail track and auto was standing just nearby. We took the auto and it drove us through the unknown part of the city. PPSC office was quite away from the usual hustle and bustle of Patiala city. The roads were silent and I was cherishing the silence all around. All I could hear was the noise from the auto's engine, which had not been serviced for quite some while. Suddenly, my mother got a call from my father. I could notice the panic in his voice but still, he was telling my mother to remain calm. I heard that and I smiled.

Horn of the train...

<u>"My father</u>

My father came from a very humble family from a village called Kang in Tarn Taran Sahib. Once as a child, I heard him saying that conditions were so worse that sometimes his grandmother had nothing to offer his father in the dinner and they had to sleep empty stomachs.

On one fine day in June 1955, CRPF came for recruitment in a nearby village. When my grandfather heard the news of recruitment, he was working barefoot on his small patch of agricultural field. He ran immediately under the scorching heat of June 12 kilometers away to the recruitment place. And, luckily he got the job.

CRPF in those times required 10.5 months posting, at a single stretch, in the tough terrains like insurgency stricken areas. Therefore, the responsibility of agriculture fell on my father. He would go to school and then work on the fields. As a child, I used to hear how he would not sleep for the entire night when his turn of 'canal water' came. Therefore in summation, his childhood was a struggle!

In 1984, my father had gone to see off his father at the Kang bus stand, hardly knowing that he would never see him again. My grandfather was posted in a very sensitive place near Agartala(Tripura) and insurgent groups were quite active in the region. One day his patrol team was surrounded in an ambush. He fought bravely and had saved the life of two of his colleagues. But in the crossfire, he was hit in his chest and soon he succumbed to his injuries. His entire career was marked with many medals and accolades.

My father was very close to him and as a child, I once saw him gazing at the photo of my grandfather and getting emotional. Time passed and after a few years of struggle, my father got a job in Chandigarh Police as a constable, and family connections led to his marriage with my mother in 1990. I often used to tease my mother and dad, that it was an impossible marital pivot, given their different socio-economic backgrounds. But one can hardly doubt, that force of time can make anything happen.

As a child, I often used to wonder why my father was so strict with me. It was strictness beyond normal. 6th Pay commission might have increased the salaries of UT policemen heftily but before that, the salary of a constable was not much to facilitate his son to study in the private schools of Chandigarh. My father somehow still managed to get me into one of the best schools in the city of those times. During my exam times, he would become a very strange, devil-like person who would beat me up for not being serious. Once he was listening to an answer and was simultaneously drinking a glass of water; I forgot a few lines and the next thing I remember is that I was drenched with water. Further, he would wake me up at 4:00 clock in the morning and we would do the second revision. Even after my exam, I had to discuss every answer with him, as to what I had written in the exam. Once, the beating got a little intense and some blood came out of my hand. My mother went wild after seeing that little scar and for the first time, I saw my mother getting infuriated and shouting at him, beyond all her limits, and my father was immediately humbled down. I enjoyed that scene! All my life I always had spoilt relations with my father, because of his acute strictness. But deep down, I knew the moving force beneath his strict attitude.

Later in my life, on the advice of a few people, I took up engineering. But I knew the history of my family and one day I came across a book on northeast insurgency and it was just the beginning. After that, I read another on Naxalism and gradually I discovered my interest in serving the insurgency stricken areas. I was good at academics, so I thought of preparing for civil services. Subsequently, I preferred not taking admission to IIT Roorkee (a very prestigious engineering institution), rather I decided to stay in my home town Chandigarh, do my graduation from PEC University, and simultaneously prepare for the Civil Service exam. And that's how the journey for civil services began in 2011."

II
CLIMBING THE WALLS

We had reached the PPSC office, the auto driver asked for an extra Rs. 100, because he knew it was my exam and my mother wouldn't refuse. My mother gave it whole heartedly and I walked away smiling. He was saying something to my mother but I couldn't hear. Later as my mother revealed, he pointed to the image of Baba Nanak in his auto and said "Bhain (sister), Nanak naam jahaz hai, chadhe so uttare paar! (Name of baba Nanak is a vehicle itself; if you travel on it you will reach destiny for sure!). Saying this he drove his auto away.

And now I stood outside the office (with a few minutes remaining). The environment outside the exam halls is always interesting moreover this was an extremely crucial stage. As usual, parents were telling some last moment words to their kids just as if the boxing coach is pressing the shoulders of the boxer, before the match. Standing there, I was noticing the walls circumscribing the PPSC office. I went closer to the wall and I noticed that there was a colony of algae on it. The dimensions of those walls and the algae gave me some déjà vu.

Horn of the train......

After my 10th class, I had taken admission in a Government senior secondary school. I had opted for a non-medical branch and in those times, our admission to engineering colleges was decided solely by a few exams like AIEEE, IIT, BITS exam, etc.

Plus two, board marks didn't count at all. But the irony was that it was expected from us to attend the school, Monday to Friday, full hours. With substandard teaching, why it was expected from us when plus two marks cannot land us anywhere, is something that still remains beyond my understanding. It was a mist of irrational demands and a mist of policy loopholes. The result was quite natural. There was an open violation of the rules. And as the governance experts have time and again said that when laws and policies are irrational, there are chances of civil disobedience, which may or may not be visible objectively. Many of my friends had taken admission into private schools, which ensured dummy attendance during admission itself. In a nutshell, these schools were charging the students, for circumventing the law grossly and openly. And vice versa, these students and their parents were paying these schools for circumventing the laws. Now here lies the core issue, which is not well thought upon. This is the age when a value regime of a person is in development mode. No matter how correct, the students and parents were. But at the unconscious level there emerges, contempt for law, and hence the "chalta hai" attitude proliferates. In later phases of life, the risk of increase in contempt, even for genuine laws becomes quite high and moreover, these students become the future engineers. We often hear about corrupt acts by engineers like deliberate use of poor material in infrastructure etc. Who knows, at what point of time the seeds of immoral behavior were sown in them!

As far as I was concerned, in such a scenario, guess what I did? I climbed the walls of my school. It was for a bunk.

I had exhausted all the legitimate means like submitting letters for leave, duly signed by my parents. My class teacher wouldn't accept it, rather would taunt me about the coaching institutes. Not because she disliked coaching, in fact, she also used to unethically give private coaching at her home (not allowed for a government teacher), but because I took Chemistry coaching from one of her market competitors. Interestingly, once I had made a school assignment and since my Chemistry coaching teacher had helped me with the required sources. I had put his name in the acknowledgment. When she opened my assignment and read his name in the acknowledgment, I swear to god, I was given the biggest cross on a single page in my entire academic life. I mean, how childish it was? I asked her, why she had put a big cross. She rebuked me and shooed me away. Not only this, the level of teaching in the school was nowhere close to what was required to clear AIEEE and IIT exams. Gradually I had become the favorite of my class teacher. She would especially track me. Once I had run away by climbing the nearby wall. This time she called my father in front of the whole class and told him about my behavior. As frustrated as I was, I entered into an argument with her. I asked her that, what alternative she had left for me. And as some ladies have the habit, she started yelling illogical things at me without giving arguments, just to dilute her frustration.

There was no logic to attend the classes in school. I didn't mend my ways and still used to run away but relations between me and my class teacher improved after I had attained the second position in the class and that too without attending her classes. I used to keep my bicycle just outside the school. From there I went straight to my home and I used to study my coaching material.

Without any doubt, policy loopholes in those times had facilitated the rise of coaching institutes. If the quality of teaching in schools was that good, why would one like to spend one lakh, per annum in these coaching institutions? It is good that since then, some reforms like the inclusion of 12th board marks for admission into the engineering colleges, have taken place but in my days, there was no alternative. Attendance was all that I came for. And as far as climbing the wall is concerned, sometimes it was quite dangerous as well. Once while climbing, I had slipped over the algae which had developed on the moist places of the walls but somehow I saved myself from falling"

And there I stood at PPSC office, standing in front of those walls and smiling at the algae of those walls.

III

ENGINEERING: THE MIST WITHIN

We then walked into the PPSC office and after some formalities and signatures, we were made to sit in a hall where our document verification was to be done. Chairman of PPSC, Lt. General Surinder Singh (retd.) visited and quite frankly he suggested us to remain calm and speak in the language of our comfort. I had decided to speak in Punjabi because not only it was my mother tongue but I was told by somebody that, it fetches greater marks in the P.C.S. interview. Further, during my document verification, the PPSC official noticed that I was wearing a turban there but in the passport size photograph I was not wearing one. He warned me that I could be grilled on this issue but I was ready with the answer. So after the document verification, we were allotted tokens and I was third to last in the sequence of interviews.

Sitting over there, I could notice the anxiety on the face and body language of other candidates. Someone was thumping his feet on the ground and one was behaving awkwardly, I mean really awkwardly. The majority of them had brought their newspapers with them and they were reading every single news piece of that day. I was looking for a chilled-out candidate and I had found one, sitting just next to me. He was quite friendly, chilled out, and a confident person. He had done engineering from a college in Hyderabad and was quite cheerful about the fact that his interview was on the second day of the entire interview schedule (of 15 days). He believed that he must have scored very good marks in the PCS mains exam to get the interview call on the second day, a notion which later on, was to prove false. Though we were told not to carry anything except documents, I had carried a bar of big chocolate hidden in my court just in case I feel hungry. We were enjoying that chocolate and suddenly he told me how his college friends are struggling to find jobs and he further said, "yaar! I think I have wasted 4 years in engineering."

Horn of the train...

Engineering, in layman's term means, using the available knowledge to create something new and innovative. There are nearly 40,000 engineering colleges in India. But the employability rate of the graduates is extremely low. And the reason is quite simple the curriculum doesn't match the demand for the required skills.

I had done mechanical engineering from PEC University of technology and somehow I had secured the second rank in the branch (with CGPA of 9.78) thanks to the notes of frontbenchers and my hard work during the last few days. But yes, I do not irk even a little to say that the ones with an average CGPA and the ones active in the Mechanical clubs were the real engineers of my branch. I was a sub-standard engineer. Those members of the mechanical clubs were even more deserving than the first ranker. They were the ones who could repair their bikes and cars and they were not like me who didn't even know how to hold a "paana". But somehow, the engineering period was a total turnaround time for me. I still remember that in the first year, my classmate and friend named Arpit used to threaten me with a boycott, if I entered the class during the "declared mass bunk". By the third year, I was threatening Arpit and a few more, with a boycott if they attended the class during the mass bunk. Times change! People Change!

And all this apart, engineering colleges are facing numerous challenges. First, in psychology, there is something called "behavioral inertia". Curriculums have not been upgraded for ages. We used to sit in labs and like stupid idiots we used to manually Xerox the text from the printed sheets, onto our files. I hardly knew what I was writing but still, I had to do it. Second, there is an acute lack of infrastructure in the colleges. Equipment is not upgraded timely and the lab machinery is defective. In the first year, there was a lab in which we had to do wiring on the wall. It felt as if the holes on the wall made by Kalpana Chawla (alumni of PEC) were still there. The wall looked that old. Thirdly, there are many loopholes in the regulatory mechanisms. And it is not a lesser-known fact that this kind of regulation has just created fertile grounds for connivance, cronyism, etc. The result was that it is easier to arrange for classic hospitality, classic dishes for the regulatory inspectors to secure UGC, AICTE accreditation than to upgrade the infrastructure. Fourthly, there is less focus on practical work. Achievements like participation and trophies in the engineering events, innovations by students, etc were not accounted for, in the academic marks. As a result, people like me just focused on theory to secure better CGPA. Fifthly, there was a lack of performance-based incentives. I had realized that ethical and hardworking teachers were being cornered in the department and internal politics and fissures were widespread. There was a teacher in our deemed University who used to allot his work of teaching to students of the class and himself used to enjoy the hospitality of backbenches. Quite confidently, many a time, he used to announce that he had no idea about the topic to be taught. And how did he get his Ph.D.? Only god knows. And as far as I was concerned, I also traveled a journey from being his good student to an outright critic of his. Moreover, why do such people get salaries of nearly 1 lakh, I again don't know. All I know is that there is a need to screen out such professors to ensure quality in engineering institutes. Moreover, in those days there was hardly any incentive for teachers to write research papers. Sixthly, there is an acute lack of linkage amongst industry, researchers, and universities. This is extremely important if universities have to become incubators of research. Sixth is willpower. During my college time, under the World Bank-funded IMPRINT scheme, we were to have online sessions with eminent faculties. We were made to sit in the auditorium many times but I had realized that it was more of a formality and not the real willpower to facilitate students to interact with those experts. Internet would not function properly and probably, just the attendance of students and associated records were enough to prove that the funds of the Government of India and World Bank are being used perfectly. Seventh, there is a lack of teacher training programs. There should be mid-career reviews, compulsory retirement in case of poor performance, grievance redressal mechanisms against the poor skills of teachers. Eighth, there are very less platforms where students can showcase their engineering innovations, and interestingly many of these innovations have huge commercial potential. In our University, we used to have capstone projects, and many students used to come out with very innovative ideas, but there was very little focus on commercializing them. Moreover, I.P.R. education was low and students didn't have much incentive. Therefore some of the great ideas kept lying in the storeroom. Engineering students have huge potential to boost the innovation capacity of our nation. But a mist is obscuring the vision of academia and needs some real focus. Therefore all these issues have created a demand-supply mismatch in the economy and hence later students regret their decision of choosing engineering as their career."

And that candidate while saying that he had wasted 4 years of engineering didn't say it just because he didn't have a job. He had a job. But just like me, he had realized quite late in his life that he was not meant for engineering; rather our real passion was civil services.

IV
CLIMBING THE HILLS

By around 12:30, the interview of four candidates was over and the fourth candidate came back to the hall. The remaining candidates saw him; they threw their newspapers away and went running towards him. All except me and my new friend were sitting on our chairs. Sitting there, we could hear him saying, "Don't do this! Don't do that!"

And,

Horn of the train ....

Dalai Lama had once said that one needs to visit a new place every year. His logic was simple. The world is too huge and one needs to witness the beauty of this planet. Therefore I had a habit of visiting a new hill station, after my UPSC exam. I preferred going all alone and I enjoyed my solitude. I found some real bliss and rejoice in the fresh air of the mountains.

While on my trek, I would cherish the sounds of birds, the noise of leaves moved by the wind. It was a kind of naturopathy. It was an escape from daily routine. UPSC preparation required 9 months of complete focus for its two stages so for the rejuvenation of my soul, mind, and body, hills were always a good escape.

In the year 2017, I went to Mcleodganj. I was excited to do a solo trek towards the Triund top. But I had not brought any accessories for trekking. Before I could begin there was a place where one had to register. I asked the person, "What was that for? "He said, "Yeh sir!! is liye, agar aap kahin kho gaye, ya kisi vajah se vapis nahi aaye, toh hum aapko dhoondhne ki koshish karenge (This because, if you don't come back or you get lost during the trek, we could send a search team to rescue you)." With these words, that man had sent a shiver deep down my spine. Anyhow, I gave my Aadhar card to him. He asked, "And who is with you?"I replied, "Nobody". He gave me a strange look as if I was some stupid who was trekking all alone. With few words: Kamaal hai sir! Dhyaan se! (amazing sir! Be careful!), he gave me the permit and during my trek, I realized that his concern was genuine. The trail was really rough and in case I twisted my feet, there was nobody there to bring me down or support me. Thereafter, I took some rest at one of the food stalls on the way. A person there was also curious about my solo trek. He warned me about the bears on this trek. Now I was getting concerned.

Until that moment, I was enjoying the scenery around me but after that I had to see towards my left time and again, into the forest area. Now I couldn't cherish the beauty around me like I was doing earlier. But in the end, everything went good and in a nutshell, I did enjoy my journey. But I came back with learning that one should not move beyond some calculated risks, but after that, you need to ignore the unnecessary threats. You need to walk with optimism, you need to be silent and avoid undue opinions of people. Sometimes you just need to let your life flow and just surrender yourself to the forces of events and time. In the end, one would realize that all the fears were useless. Moreover, if we respect nature, nature respects us back. When I came back, my mother showed me a piece of news in the newspaper. It was about a Russian man who had died on the Triund trek due to a heart attack. Somehow I took the scolding of my mother with a smile but a simple thing is that one should always be aware of one's limitations, one's capacity, no matter whether it's a real journey up the hill or some journey or some struggle in your life.

After that, it was the year 2018 and I went to Dalhousie, Khajjiar, and Chamba. It was a new place, a new hill and a new trek. A famous trek near Dalhousie is called "Dainkund trek". There is a single taxi company over there and it has allied with every possible local vendor and shopkeeper, to make us believe that no HRTC bus goes to the base of the trek and that it's kind of a compulsion to hire a taxi till the base point. I met a tax-owner there and he tried to make me believe the same. Lesser he knew that I was preparing for UPSC for the last 7 years and I was sure that it was just not possible, that a socialist state like ours doesn't run a bus service to every possible nook and corner of our nation. As it came out, I met a tourist there, he told me that the bus was to arrive at 2:00 PM and there were, in fact, many more services after that. The taxi driver was asking for Rs 900 to drop me at "Lakkad mandi" (from where the trek is quite close). But via bus, I had reached there at a nominal charge of Rs 15. It was a great deal for me after all I was unemployed. Similarly, in our life also, there is a mist of illusions created by different forces, different vested interests, and different idiots of some very high order around us. We just need to have the vision to look beyond, a vision to see the reality, a vision to find the best possible way out. But the most interesting part, while on my bus to Lakkad mandi, I entered into a conversation with a fellow traveler of some old age. I asked him why this trek is called "Dainkund trek" and with a strange look on his face, he said that at the top of the hill a "Dayan" (witch) was burnt by local people. But before he said anything else, I just plugged my earphones and started listening to songs. I swear on god, if I would have carried the conversation further, he would have told me that the spirit of "Dayan" still roams around there. I just recalled my Triund experience, and preferred silence. And about the trek, it was a beautiful trek with some majestic views from there. There were many tourists on the top. Some of them were doing yoga there. Just nearby, there was a panel stating a beautiful quote "Pahadhon me shudh vaayu aur Vaayu se aayu (Get pure air in the mountains and enhance your life)". I took a nap on that grass and it was a great memory. The distance from Lakkad mandi to the top of the trek was around 6km. It was steep and tiring. But the journey was worth it. Moreover, I had clicked a picture from the Dainkund hilltop and that picture was to become my laptop wallpaper (which meant it was to be there in front of me every day, for the next 9 months of my preparation). During my 5th attempt at UPSC civil service examination, whenever I looked at that wallpaper scenery, it reminded me of the efforts of my climb with due optimism. Without any doubt, optimism and faith provide us the required fuel to tread difficult paths; to chalk out our ways through the mist of dire circumstances.

But the trip wasn't over yet. After the Dainkund trek, on the 3rd day of my trip I went to Chamba. There is a famous early medieval temple called Chamundaaya temple there.

Being a student of history, I was curious to visit that place. It was located midway up the hill and there were two ways to go. First, there were 378 steps, carved on the hill, and each step was quite huge, unlike the ones that we use in our homes. Hence it was a difficult route and a difficult climb. The second was an easier one, a slanted road, over which one could walk, hire a taxi, etc. But I had chosen the path of 378 steps. One will definitely run out of breath on this path but as you go up, the majestic view of Chamba valley along the Ravi River keeps on becoming more and more beautiful. Later I realized that this view couldn't be seen on that swirling road as the view is blocked by the intermediate hills. Therefore there are paths in our lives that are a little difficult, a little risky, but sometimes both destination and journey, are extremely beautiful. In that small climb, a person who took a taxi or who had walked on that slant road, to reach that temple was not as lucky as me. Therefore difficult seeming paths are sometimes preferable and must be opted for.

Subsequently, in 2019, I had gone to different places in Tirthan valley. But this time, with my cousin. He also wanted an escape from the monotony of work life. We went to an off-beat location called Jibhi. It is a beautiful place with an exotic waterfall, from which a rainbow emerges. Near to that place lies Jalori pass, and a trek to Raghupur fort begins from that pass only. The fort was built by rulers of Mandi and a unique feature of the hill forts throughout history was that they were always built on the hilltop to prevent the invasion of the enemy. Further, the height of the fort was a challenge as it was 3200 meters plus. As usual, we started the trek. We walked for around 2 kilometers on a trail that went through the mountain jungle. Just before the point from where two - three routes parted away; there was a small Bugyal (a flat grassy region). Since there were no markings, we became a little confused and therefore we asked a person about the right trail to the fort. He was sitting and smoking (I don't know what). He didn't speak but just pointed towards one of the routes and we started walking. We walked for 2-3 kilometers but there was no one around us (these were pre corona times) and we started having a doubt. But somehow we kept walking and we reached a small lake, with some locals sitting nearby. They belonged to a nearby village and we asked them about the fort. They looked at each other and told us the very point from where we took the wrong route. We looked at each other and started laughing. That stupid person had guided us the wrong way and he was stoned. Nevertheless, that place was a beautiful hilly pasture, with cows grazing over it and we had an opportunity to see a rare hilly lake and a geomorphologic feature called "centripetal drainage" about which I had only read in my geography book. Then we finally traveled back those 2-3 kilometers and we again started a steep climb and this time along the right path. The sun was setting and we finally reached the top. It was a beautiful landscape. Trees were absent and lush green grass could be seen everywhere but the fort was still not visible and there were rather small chowkis (built of stones). I got some déjà vu yet again, as in our upward ascent; we had heard a descending group saying that they were being fooled in the name of the fort as there was no fort there and rather some stone jhonpadis. Probably they mistook those small chowkis as the remnants of the fort. We both were also confused as to where the hell was the fort. Moreover, it was Monday and there were very few tourists around and that too at distant places. Having climbed that hill, after walking the wrong path, we were acutely tired and I had a gut feeling that the fort was nearby. It was a little misty out there and things were not clearly visible. We moved further on that Bugyal and we saw a group of trekkers coming from a distance, towards us. They told us that the fort was a little further. So in sum, even after reaching the top, one had to walk over 3 small slant hills, to get to the fort. I was thinking that those people walking down the hill had reached so near to that fort, still, they missed it. Similarly in life, we make tremendous efforts to reach our goals. But in the end, either due to poor judgments or wrong guidance we tend to give up in the face of exhaustion or we fail to realize that the last step is the most crucial one and sometimes also the most difficult one.

So in the next few minutes, we were standing in front of the fort. My cousin warned me that the sun was setting and walking through the forest in dark could be dangerous. I agreed, but before leaving we walked on walls of fortification of that fort. It gave us the feeling that we had dared to reach that place. We had seen every corner of the fort, step-wells built inside it. But the effects of the force of nature and time were visible on that fort.

Therefore be it the Triund trek, Dainkund trek, Chamba, or the Raghubar fort trek, there were few learnings from all these experiences. First, you should always start your journey with a fresh mindset. Second, beware of the misguidance at the crucial stages of your life. Third, the risks you take should be calculated, and once you do that you need not pay heed to excessive cautions and warnings because we are all different and the world is every ready to give you warnings and induce unnecessary fear in you"

And there I sat in that hall watching him tell precautions and the dos and the don'ts and those candidates were listening to him very carefully as if his words were some cheat codes.

(Moreover, as it later came out, neither that candidate nor the one listening to him got selected and in fact, all of them performed quite poorly in the interview). For me it was quite simple, my Himachal diaries didn't allow me to listen to his cautions and precautions and I wanted to go fresh into the interview. Moreover, sometimes the biggest source of confidence is the acceptance of uncertainty. Nothing can surpass that kind of confidence!

V

THE INTERVIEW

The interview of many candidates was over and now it was the turn of my friend. So he went in and next was my turn. While leaving the hall I noticed that the last women candidate was feeling a little nervous and was walking quite fast, in the almost empty room now. I wished her the best. I was now sitting on the chair just outside the interview room. The peon was sitting in front of me and I had a nice good talk with him. He was in his 50's and was very cheerful. He asked me how was I feeling and I replied that there were some butterflies in my stomach. He said that was fine and he went running to a nearby room and brought a water bottle for me. Meanwhile, my friend came out and was feeling confident. He wished me luck and told me that he would wait outside for me. I had to enter the room after 5 minutes. I looked at the peon uncle and said, "Uncle asheerwad deoh(Give me your blessings uncle)". He smiled and paused for a while and said, "Beta tu zaroor officer banega. Hajje tak kisi ne wi iss kursi te baith ke mere naal is taraah gal nahi kiti. Rab tere naal ahi beta(You will surely be an officer son. Till now nobody has talked to me sitting on this chair, the way you did. God is with you)."

I then walked into the room. It was a rectangular room and 10 bureaucrats were sitting on chairs lined up along 3 sides of the room in front of me was the chairman of PPSC, Lt. General (retd) Surinder Singh.

I greeted the panel and took my seat.

Lt. General Sir: *Kaaka, here you are wearing a turban and in this photograph, you are not. What is this? Yours is a split personality. Many panel members agreed to him, and some of them even laughed and taunted, while some of them posed me related questions simultaneously....*

Me: *Sir I will honestly confess that before 2019 I had never worn a turban. (Silence followed!)*

A Panelist: *Then why today?*

Another Panelist: *What happened in 2019?*

Horn of the train.......

"For most of my life I had been an agnostic person with a tilt towards atheism, I had never given any importance to the wearing of religious symbols. But in 2019 I was reading a book by Khushwant Singh i.e. history of Sikhs and I had read the period of Zakariya Khan(Governor of Lahore), a phase following the death of Banda Singh Bahadur when there were 'almost' shoot at sight orders on those Sikhs who wore a turban. Sikhs remained fearless and openly disobeyed his orders. That was a heritage to feel proud of and for the first time I had worn a turban at a formal occasion in the year 2019."

Me: *I spoke briefly about my experience with Khuswant Sir's book.*

Panelist: *If that's the case I will ask a faculty to recommend you another book and maybe you will become Khalsa also? You may. Isn't it?*

Me: *Sir becoming a Khalsa is a big step. I cannot commit anything right now. But I will think about it.*

Lt. General Sir: *Soothing down the tense questioning atmosphere. So tell me if you are posted in a district what will be your 3 priorities. (Actually, he used a tough synonym for the word "priorities" but I couldn't understand, so I had to say, "I beg your pardon I didn't get it". Then he simplified the word. The usage was intentional)*

_Me_: *Sir Education, Health and skills.*

Lt. General Sir: *And the order?*

_Me_: *Sir first education, then health, and then skills*

Panelist: *Some engineering-based questions (replied quite well).*

Lt. General Sir: *How will you reform the health system of Punjab. Tell me the dimensions cross Problems, challenges, and solutions*

_Me_ :

Sir regarding Problems :

- *Patient to bed ratio is quite low i.e.1.2 per 1 lakh.*
- *Doctor to patient ratio is just 0.7 per 1000.*
- *Just 550 medical colleges are there in India as compared to 45000 engineering colleges.*
- *Low awareness of insurance and loopholes in RSBY and Ayushman scheme, hence high out-of-pocket spending.*

Lt General Sir: *And challenges?*
_Me_ :

- *Financial constraints: Punjab's health budget is quite low at 4600 crores.*
- *Faith of village people in Quacks (gave example of my village).*
- *Stubble burning and asthma.*
- *Polluted groundwaters and cancer in the Malwa region.*

- *Drug issues.*

Lt. General Sir: *and Solutions?*
Me :

- *More no. of mohalla clinics (Delhi and Cuban model of health).*
- *Telehealth should be given focus.*
- *Better infrastructure in Primary Health centers.*
- *More no. of medi-cities like Mullanpur*

Lt. General Sir: *Stops me; extended his hand and rubbed his thumb against two fingers and then made a hand gesture of "how".*
Me :
Sir the most important way of finance mobilization is that we save upon excessive and irrational expenditure for example charging rich farmers for electricity; subsidy rationing etc
   Alongside,

- *Canceling licenses of private companies, enrolled in the Ayushman scheme if they are found guilty of leakages.*
- *Incentives to the companies for routing their C.S.R funds in the health sector.*
- *Need of a state health cess.*
- *Health bonds.*

Lt. General Sir: *Jashan!!..pauses (first time in 7-10 minutes I noticed some softness in his voice), you have scored 9.78 CGPA and that too in PEC university of technology. Why are you here?*
Me: *Sir after I was elected as the head boy in my 10th class, Principal Madam called me in her office and she took a promise from me that I would not become a doctor or an engineer, as*

they were enough of them out there. I promised that I will become a teacher or a bureaucrat. But sir, I broke her promise and I opted for engineering as my parents demanded that. I got selected in IIT Roorkee (2011) but I decided to stay in Chandigarh and took admission in PEC so that I could live the dream of my principal and also uphold the legacy left by my grandfather. Now I teach whenever I am free and I have been preparing for the civil service exam as well.

Panelist: You have filled "security" as an area of interest why?

Horn of the train......

"My father once told me that had your grandfather not died fighting the insurgents, you would have been studying in a village school and I wouldn't have been there in Chandigarh. Therefore my interest in the issue of insurgencies gradually increased. Moreover, I had read many books on North East insurgency, Naxalism, and Punjab insurgency. Subsequently, I had written many articles on these issues for The Tribune and The Hindu. In 2016, when I had to fill the order of state preferences for the UPSC civil service exam, I had filled North East states first, without telling my father".

_Me_: Sir my Grandfather had laid his life while fighting the Rebels of Tripura (answered a few questions following that)

Lt. General Sir: You have written that you are writing your book. What is the title and what is it about?

_Me_: The title shall be probably "A climb through the Mist" and it is about my struggles and experiences

Lt. General Sir: (with a hand gesture), but who will read your book?

_Me_: Sir those who are struggling and are looking for some motivation, will read this book.

Lt. General Sir: I mean what if you don't succeed?

<u>Me</u>: *I will surely succeed sir. I have spent 9 years of my life in civil service exam preparation. (Actually, I got a little strong in this answer, and post the interview I was in doubt whether I had been a little overconfident)*

<u>Panelist</u>: *What should be the role of society towards a struggling person?*

<u>Me</u>: *Society should motivate such people; must be compassionate; give them time and space just like the way Japanese society does.*

<u>Panelist</u>: *Do you think, people here don't do that?*

<u>Me</u>: *No ma'am (I heard another panelist say "sahi gal hai / that's right") but ma'am, few people are always there who motivate us (as I had some people in my mind including the peon uncle sitting outside).*

<u>Panelist</u>: *Asked me some questions on International relations and I answered very well but as she asked some more questions, another panelist interrupted (maybe it was a test of the presence of mind)...*

<u>Different Panelist</u>: *Bureaucracy is facing many problems; it is almost synonymous with red-tapism. Will you like to say something?*

<u>Me</u>: *Definitely sir and I went back to the previous panelist as her questions regarding groundwater and health were still not answered. After I answered her, I came back to sir and said, "Sir I beg your pardon, bureaucracy is not synonymous with Red tapism. No doubt, the problem is still there but we have many solutions like creating a strict time limit of 21 days after which bureaucrats should be punished without inquiry; implementing the recent Punjab Anti Red tape Act 2020; certainty and not extremity in the punishment; citizen charters, etc".*

<u>The same Panelist</u> : *(Citing the name of a national leader) he had said something not so good (and he specified also) about the bureaucrats. Are you aware that he said this?*

Horn of the train.....

"In the interest section of my form, it was only the political field that I had not ticked. I had ticked every single interest and I wrote some more interests in the margin, so I thought, maybe he was testing me."

Me: *I am not aware of it sir (The truth is that I was aware, but had I said that, he would have asked more political questions and a bureaucrat can never talk about his political opinions openly as per the code of conduct rules).*

Panelist: *Laughed (and other panelists laughed with him).*

Panelist: *But it was widely published in the newspapers and everybody here is aware of it?*

Me: *Sir but I am not aware of it.*

Panelist: *But do you agree with what he said?*

Me: *Not at all sir.*

Lt. General sir: *Alright Jashan. Thank you*

Me: *Thank you (and I walked out confidently)*

I told peon uncle sitting outside, that the interview was good. I took his blessings again and I walked out of the gate. My mother was on a phone call and the other side of the call it was my maternal uncle (maamaji).

Horn of the train...

"I and my brother had always shared a very strong bond with him. Two days before while talking to me, he told me that I had to live the dream of my maternal grandfather. Though it was a different thing that I had always wanted to serve in North East on lines of paternal grandfather, but as destiny would have it, my UPSC attempts were exhausted by then. "

He had called my mother 4 times just during the last 25-30 minutes of the interview. I had not even finished telling my experience to my mother and few people approached me to enquire as to what was asked in the interview. Actually, sisters of both had to appear in the interview 4 days thence, and they had planted them in the front gate to pass the cheat codes or the intelligence information. I wanted to suggest to them, to let their sisters go afresh without any expectations for the interview but then I thought they will misunderstand me. So I told them everything, paid farewell to my friend and we left for Chandigarh.

VI

THE PINDARIS

I was sitting in the car, with a strange peace. It had not been a smooth day and as we were traveling back from Patiala I recalled a place and also a street vendor standing there as 2 months ago I was in Patiala for 8 days and I had asked him the location of Gandhi Lake (near which my hotel was located), as Google map was not working properly. I had stayed in a hotel named Godwin. In April, we had to appear for a written exam for 7 consecutive days. I would take an auto every day to my exam hall (Khalsa College). I could still recall the unique taste of that hotel's food even then. Moreover, out of 60,000 candidates who had appeared for the preliminary exam earlier in February, just 800 had made it to the main written exam in April. And now, while traveling back in that car, I knew that I was competing with just 175 people in Punjab, for the final 16 seats (general category male candidates).

We were back on our way and the road from Patiala to Chandigarh is much better than it was in 2016. In 2016, I and 3 of my friends used to travel every day from Chandigarh to Patiala by bus for writing the PCS mains exam and the roads in some parts of the journey were in horrible condition. But now, one could reach Chandigarh in an hour or so and hence it was a smooth drive. In the initial part of the journey; we discussed the interview quite curiously and after that my mother and Harwinder ji told me that in the morning, the tire of the car had got punctured just 4-5 kilometer away from Patiala, but somehow I didn't notice it but they two knew but they didn't tell me. We had good laughs and in the latter part of the journey, there was silence in the car as everyone was a little exhausted. I was looking outside and one advertisement repeated again and again. It was that of a civil service coaching institute.

Horn of the train......

In medieval India, Pindaris were first heard during the late 17th century. They were irregular horsemen of Maratha armies. Once Maratha armies were disbanded following the Treaty of Bassein (1802), they became freelance. Gradually they took to plunder. Pindaris formed a composite class of different sections, different religions, all united with just one purpose i.e. plunder. But they had their code of conduct. They were known for their professional integrity and they had principles even in plunder. And today no doubt some coaching institutions continue to be ethical and are guiding students effectively but some of them are acutely unethical, unprofessional, and don't have a code of conduct like the 19th-century Pindaris. These institutions are a manifestation of "get rich quick syndrome", which has infested our society quite deeply.

Not to talk about other fields, if civil service exam alone is considered, coaching has become such an attractive industry that some UPSC aspirants who had never reached the interview stage or even had reached the mains stage just once or twice are posing as some expert teachers and have even set up their coaching institutions. Moreover, in our cultural heritage, students have been always taught to give respect and touch the feet of a guru. But the issue is that in the Vedic times, education was almost free and now the coaching institutes are charging up to 1.5 lakh-2 lakh for the entire civil service course. They are more like service providers and students are more like consumers. And with the heritage of touching the feet of a Guru and not questioning much, students sometimes don't even think whether the teacher is even capable of teaching or not. They are afraid of having a debate/dialogue with the teacher on key issues just because their guru may feel offended.

The issue with these substandard teachers is that they just don't know the difference between the "civil service exam" style of teaching and the "graduation course" style of teaching. They have their limitations. It might be very interesting for students to hear stories from these people but that is just not required in the civil service exam and this, the students realize quite later. Moreover, these substandard teachers do nothing more than create a replica of them amongst the students. In a nutshell, sometimes "a student pays heftily to get misguided" and hence they spoil their career.

Not only this, some of these institutes and teachers even recommend unnecessary books; they provide redundant notes because they have to justify the hefty fee, they are charging. But in reality, the real requirement and a simple requirement is to deliver a comprehensive and holistic set of notes beyond which students need not study much at home. A teacher must amalgamate all the information from different sources and deliver these notes so that a student could just revise them and do the answer writing practice at home. But many of them don't do that because of two reasons. First, because they fear that their notes might get leaked into the market, and second such notes don't justify the hefty fee they are charging right now.

Not only this, they have become acutely shameless in manipulating the results through which they market themselves. With the manipulation of results, there is a lack of accountability of these institutes and they can sustain their business even with false yet aggressive marketing. Once I was sitting with one such a Pindari, and quite proudly he told me that he purchases the results from toppers. By saying that he meant, when a candidate gets selected, he pays that candidate to give her passport-sized photo for the toppers list of coaching institutes, while he may have never taught that candidate. And some of them have found a new way, i.e. of using a single photo 2-3 times in their list of selected candidates because a bulky list can easily be monetized in the market. Similarly, another way is that of collaboration. A coaching institute collaborates (just for namesake) with other institutes in Delhi or some other cities, and the selected candidates of one institute automatically become the golden candidates of the other institution, and interestingly the candidates themselves might have never heard about such institutes. Another hilarious yet reckless way is that some north Indian institutes just copy-paste the pics of south Indian selected candidates, from some websites. The lesser we speak of them the better it is. Another way is that during interview preparation if a candidate attends the 30-minute mock interview with them, then he/she automatically becomes their golden student (in case he gets selected). All this is a part of "get rich quick syndrome".

If I were to ask as to what would be a genuine result of an institution, I will say that when a hardworking candidate after the right guidance across all the three stages, clears the exam in a maximum of 2 attempts, only then these institutes have the right to claim him/her

Another question is why these institutes are proliferating at such a high rate. It is because of the rising demand and aspirations of students to become a bureaucrat. But then why is there a massive demand? My story had begun from the office of my school principal and the motivation, I got from my grandfather, but there are some more interesting and unique reasons, I had come across. The reason, first of all, lies in our society where sometimes the middle class, lower-middle-class, and poor are not treated well in society. They have to face a lot of harassment in the government offices, government hospitals and where not? Therefore the desire emerges for "ijjat (respect)", "less harassment" and "higher status" and therefore the love for "batti waali gaadis". Not only this, there are many other reasons too. Once an aspirant openly accepted in front of me that he wanted to become a bureaucrat because he wanted to do a lot of corruption and even surpass his relative (a corrupt bureaucrat) in material possessions. Further, one said, "he wanted to teach his "taaya (elder brother of father), a lesson!". But yes definitely, I have also met aspirants who could have opted for a comfortable job and life, but they wanted to become a bureaucrat just out of their passion for social service. In summation, numerous reasons have pushed up the demand for guidance for the civil service exam and hence the tremendous rise of coaching institutes.

Not to say that situation is abysmal, there are good coaching institutes also. Further these days, online free coaching services are also provided (though the human psyche is such that free things are not valued much). Therefore there is a need for greater vigilance while choosing coaching institutions. Moreover, self-study is also a good option if one has a credible source of guidance as a lot of top rankers have cleared exams just via self-study. Finally, these coaching institutes need to self introspect.

VII
THE VANISHING MEMORY

We came back home, I met my dad and I then went into my paternal grandmother's room who was in Chandigarh, for the last couple of months. I touched her feet and she asked me, "Beta Khet nu paani laa dita hai (Have you irrigated the field)?". I paused for a while and said, "haanji beeji(yes grandmother)".

Horn of the train.................

I had always remembered her as a short and frail woman since childhood. Grandfather had died in 1984 and all the responsibilities fell on her. She was a very introverted lady, talked very little, and she had a strong sense of attachment with our village house in the district Tarn Taran Sahib. As a child also, whenever she visited our house in Chandigarh, she would always be in a hurry to go back. For the last couple of years, she was suffering from progressive dementia because of which the memory of a person vanishes gradually. She visited my home in March and I was all wiped out from her memories, though she remembered my father.

I would try to recall her about my name and some days she could and on some days she just couldn't. Not only this, she was forgetting how to eat and my father had to teach her. She had forgotten the name of dals and vegetables but she remembers her favorite mangoes. Since she is quite close to my cousin living in Tarn Taran, that is the only name she remembers properly and whenever she needed some help, she would shout his name. Once I was passing across her room and she was looking down the bed quite vigorously. I asked," What happened Beeji?" She said, "Dog is below this bed and it is troubling me." There was no dog. And one day she was trying to pluck the painted flowers from the bedsheet and since she wasn't able to pluck them, she called me for help. Similarly, whenever she would sit on the balcony, she would refer every passing street vendor, by the name of her village vegetable seller. One day I was asleep in my room, and at 3:00 AM she came into my room quietly, stood near me and shouted the name of my cousin, and said, " Utth ja!!pasuan di dhaar choni hai (Wake up, we have to milk the cows). I got scared to hell! And then I gently escorted her back to her room saying, "haanji beeji main cho dina haan (Sure Beeji, I will do it)." And the incident repeated once again when I was asleep, but this time the story was different.

And one day she was sitting in bed and singing Punjabi Lok geet (folk songs). I went to her and asked her, "you don't remember my name but you remember these geets. This is interesting!"She said, "No beta, I remember your name." I said, "Then tell me please!". She then put her hand on my head and then rubbed it gently and said, "Your name is...... Gurjant Singh Kang (my cousin's name)". I laughed, folded my hands, touched her feet and I sat down to listen to her interesting talks. Seeing her, I would often think that there is not much difference between childhood and senile age."

VIII

ELECTRONIC MEDIA AND THE MIST

After that, I walked into the dining room and my brother had already ordered my favorite dish. We were discussing the interview; my brother (pursuing MBBS at that time) suggested me some good points in the health sector questions and then scolded me as to how could I miss those points. "Please bro, let me have my food", I said. Suddenly I switched on the television. A news channel was presenting the top 100 news of the day. 90% of the content was related to the Coronavirus and the rest 10% included silly and trivial stuff.

Horn of the train........

Media: the new mist

I once wrote a poem

The 4ᵗʰ pillar of democracy, and flag-bearer of free speech,

The powerful fear its scrutiny, with the scope of its reach,
Information, education and what not does it provide,
But are those ways,........ right?
From information provider to perception developer,
Molding the news for some perpetrators,
TRP Races and the sensationalism,
The crisis of ethics and the yellow journalism,
Post-truth, fake news, and the hype
High decibel debates, but the rarity of the "Ravish style"
Look at the Press freedom index and tell me: Why this poor plight.

A simple question is why media is so important and what is the mist all about? As a citizen of this nation, my opinions, my ideologies, my perspectives every day are shaped by the happenings all around and media plays like a link in communicating those happenings to me every day. Hence it has a huge role in everybody's life but the issue is about truth, fairness, and bias. The media is definitely in a state of crisis.

It has created a mist and the mist doesn't let the people around, analyze the core issues facing them. This mist is limiting our vision, our horizons of thinking and it is restricting the people to some narrow trivial topics. For example, Hindu-Muslim debates, controversies around Tipu Sultan, why a CM deliberately doesn't grow hair on his head, do aliens drink cow milk, and numerous other rubbish topics, have found half an hour or even full one hour space in the news debates and discussions. Not only this, media houses behave like sycophants many a time who sing to the tune of the ruling party and this is not a new phenomenon.

There are numerous reasons for this mist. First is the separation of ownership and editorial. The owners of media houses many a time have political allegiances and the owner can twist the news presented on his/her channel and therefore a bias emerges. Second is the political victimization. Ravish Kumar, Ramon Magsaysay winner, in his book "the free voice", had pointed out several astonishing facts. Constructive criticism is the duty of any media house in a democracy but unfortunately, there is targeted victimization of ethical journalists. These journalists are the ones who dare to question, who dare to talk about core issues facing the nation. Third, the T.R.P. races. In a world of numerous news channels, there is a race to fetch maximum viewership and fetch higher TRPs. Higher TRPSs would fetch them more no. of advertisements and with the finance flowing through advertisements, it becomes possible to run and sustain a media house. But the issue is that at unconscious levels, we people have supported media in its focus on trivial issues. The human psyche is such that, sensational news, high decibel debates, shouting, fighting fetches greater attention. This has pushed news channels to focus on trivial topics. Debates are held amongst some illiterate babas, maulvis, etc rather than intellectuals. These illiterate people shout, fight, slap each other and yes they help news channels, in fetching the viewership of people and hence the rise in TRPs. Fourth is poor accountability. It is very easy for a news channel to present fake news and get away with it. News presenters are not held accountable. The news of chip in Rs 2000 note was widely popularized. But nobody was held accountable for spreading this news. PCI has very limited powers in regulating media. NBSA and ASCI have their own problems. Fifth, ground reporters, news presenters, debate moderators have their own biases and that is manifested in their news reporting. Sixth is related to our general way of life. Superstitions are still widely believed in our society and hence there have been 1-hour shows of some Babas (self-proclaimed saints) on the news channels, which I used to see as comedy shows. How can a news channel give space to Babas who believe that if we consume green chutney (sauce) instead of red chutney, then god's grace will fall upon us? Seventh, even political parties have indirect ownerships in news channels. How can such news channels be unbiased and fair enough with other political parties? Eighth is about cheap news. For covering the core issues facing the nation, news channels need many ground reporters to travel in the backward and rural areas. That requires an expenditure on petrol; on the salary of news reporters; a risk that even after traveling to core areas, one may not find sufficient quality and quantity of news. Hence some sensational, eye-catching news already present on the internet, is given some decent space on news platforms. Hence the attention of people is diverted from core issues.

This kind of mist is really dangerous. Hindu Muslim debates are increasing the levels of fundamentalism. People remain ignorant about the key issues and this process is further diluting the value of compassion towards fellow beings. Our fundamental duties direct us to develop scientific temperament, but superstitions are being spread by the very 4th pillar of democracy. Further, making autonomous choices while voting has become a little difficult because sometimes pre-polls are deliberately distorted in favor of parties to which the media house owes its allegiance. Hence some media houses play the role of perception developers rather than truth-tellers. Moreover, if there is no constructive criticism of the government, how can the government of the day improve its policies? And some sycophant media houses play no substantive role in that direction. Further, children and adolescents learn what they see. By observing short-tempered people in news debates, they learn all those vices. Moreover, there are news anchors in a debate, who speak more and listen less, or listen to only that stuff which they want to listen and English is still considered as a superior language in India and when anchors talk in English, Indian people look up to their mess and have even become fans of these silly news anchors. With their power of influence, they create similar clones in the society and there is already enough population of stupid people on this planet. We don't need more of them.

Whenever I used to watch these T.V. news channels, I virtually tried to find my way out through the mist of wholesome crap. I must say that genuine efforts are being made in form of self-funded channels and also towards independent journalism. Very senior and eminent journalists who don't find a place in the sycophant media houses now have their youtube channels. It is totally fine for journalists to take sides, rather it is important to take sides. But this should take place only after rigorous analysis of authentic evidence. People have right over their own opinions, not their own facts."

IX

A WALK TO REMEMBER : LIFE BEYOND THE MIST OF IGNORANCE

I have a habit of going for an evening walk but that day I was a little exhausted but still, I went. It was not my usual walk in the nearby park rather a roadside walk and where I did that I always used to talk to random street vendors. That day I came across a rikshawala. On the side of a small chowk of sectors 18-D and 18-A of Chandigarh, he was sitting on his rikshaw and was submerged into some deep thinking.

Most of such vendors and rikshaw pullers are migrants. They feel very good if you stop by and talk about their lives and village. The reason is that in big cities, they are considered as working machines or mere tools of these fast-moving lives.

Therefore sometimes they feel deprived of the human element. So as I had started talking about his background and his village, there was a unique smile on his face. He was originally from U.P. His wife lived back in his village and had 2 kids who were studying in the village school. Every week or fortnight he deposited the surplus money in his bank account and then his wife used to withdraw. That day he had made some average money. We talked and as usual like many others he had small dreams, small worries, and some perspectives which were strongly restricted by his hand-to-mouth living. We talked for nearly 15-20 minutes and he even offered me a discount on his rickshaw fares. I laughed and thanked him. I had told him nothing about my interview or my efforts to become a bureaucrat but still as I was leaving he offered me a free ride back to my home but I gently refused. He didn't amaze me with his kind gesture because such gestures can easily be found in the lower rungs of society as compared to the socio-economically well-off people.

As I walked back I pondered upon his words

Horn of the train.....

- Area of earth = 5500 million square km
- The population of humans = 7 billion
- Age of earth = 4.543 billion years
- The average life expectancy of humans presently = taking the average, let's say around 60

I have deliberately quoted these out of context, seeming facts here to point out two things. First, the length of our life is extremely, extremely short (Kindly look at the age of the earth and you will realize), while the breadth of our life is huge (see the area of earth and scope of reach of an average human in his lifetime). Second, we people never realize that we are so lucky, that we are born at the peak of human civilization, a civilization that took 4.534 billion years to evolve. We are those lucky ones who are enjoying the best facilities one can get.

But suddenly one hears about, an eminent person called K Siddhartha jumping off the bridge for some reason. Sometimes one hears about an adolescent committing suicide, sometimes we attach ourselves so much to some people or some petty issues of life that it affects our peace of mind. As already depicted, many of us do not live our dreams. But we get absorbed into the average life, presented by society. Moreover, let's stay away from the capitalism or communism debate. But I have observed that some unethical factory owners or company owners almost try to enslave people. They openly violate the labor laws, employ child labor, and extract a daily work of 12-13 hours from laborers. The result is, such people, do not have time to even appreciate the worth of life. They become virtual machines and once they get stuck in this mist, their vision becomes narrow and their perspectives get parochial, and from here on begins the demise of their potential dreams. There is a strange entrapment that is silent and invisible. A person throughout one's life is a prisoner of somebody else, of the boss, of one's petty thoughts, and may be of one's own emotions. There is a kind of self-imposed imprisonment.

And a strange irony was that, for the last 7 years, I had spent most of my life in my room, preparing for my dream job, enough for my friends, relatives, neighbors to call me a crazy prisoner. Hardly had they known that sitting in my room I was way freer than them. I was pursuing my dream, out of my own will, a will not be imposed by anybody. I went to sleep happy and awoke with passion because I was at least chasing my passion. Many people do not dare to liberate themselves from their self-incurred handicaps. They live in an illusion, that they are free. But they are not. They are more mobile but not free.

By god's grace, my parents earned enough, to give me a quality life, while I was chasing my dreams. I agree that in many homes, conditions are such that a person may be forced to take up a job which he/she may not like. But the real problem is not with them but with those people, who have all the avenues and resources at their command, and still, out of acute shortsightedness, they willfully surrender themselves to an average or sub-standard "social suction pump". Therefore if it is possible, risk should be taken and goals should be set as per one's passion. And what if, we fail in the end? Who can snatch away the satisfaction from us that we had dared to struggle; we had dared to follow a road less traveled; we had dared to leave an inspiration for many more to come. Moreover, a few stanzas of the poem of H.W. Longfellow i.e. Psalm of life go like this:-

Tell me not, in mournful numbers,
Life is but an empty dream!—
For the soul is dead that slumbers,
And things are not what they seem.
Life is real! Life is earnest!
And the grave is not its goal;
Dust thou art, to dust returnest,
Was not spoken of the soul.
Not enjoyment, and not sorrow,
Is our destined end or way;
But to act, that each to-morrow
Find us farther than today.
Art is long, and Time is fleeting,
And our hearts, though stout and brave,
Still, like muffled drums, are beating

Funeral marches to the grave.
In the world's broad field of battle,
In the bivouac of Life,
Be not like dumb, driven cattle!
Be a hero in the strife!
Trust no Future, however pleasant!
Let the dead Past bury its dead!
Act,—act in the living Present!
Heart within, and God overhead!
The lives of great men all remind us
We can make our lives sublime,
And, departing, leave behind us
Footprints on the sands of time;
Footprints, that perhaps another,
Sailing o'er life's solemn main,
A forlorn and shipwrecked brother,
Seeing shall take heart again.
Let us, then, be up and doing,
With a heart for any fate;
Still achieving, still pursuing,
Learn to labor and to wait.

Moving ahead I have also seen people spoiling their well-being by strongly attaching themselves to some people or some things. Life is too short, way too short for that. They say magnanimity is a very good value. It is, in fact, true but no one is worth that much, that you let them spoil your peace of mind. One thing that life has taught all these years is that you cannot be good all the time. One must realize that some thoughts, some emotions, some people are not worth even a cent in your life.

Not only this, during my struggle or preparation phase, I had realized the importance of small things in life. I had kept my study table quite close to the windowpane of my room. On the other side, I kept a bowl full of bird feed. While studying, sometimes I would look at birds feeding on the food. I started cherishing the beauty of lush green trees outside.

We are not immortal. One has to realize this fact deeply. It is not a depressing fact. But when one realizes that we are not going to live forever on this planet, we start looking at things differently. We start cherishing small things. We start letting go of, the stupid and petty things much more easily. But then the issue is, many people think that they are at the center of the universe. It is just not like that. We are tiny species on this planet. The problems in our life are not because of those external things, but just because of our estimate of them. The problem starts in our mind and it has to end there only.

Then let's talk about gratitude. It is the parent of all the virtues. If you have that a trek in solitude through the hills becomes more blissful; we start appreciating the hug from your near and dear ones and stars in the sky become more beautiful. I mean, ask yourself when did you get out alone in the night, on the top of your house and you cherished the stars in the sky while standing alone. Isn't the answer, "Life is too busy for that kind of stuff?" The truth is that adversities can never overwhelm a person who has the value of gratitude and who understands the value of gratitude. The unearned increments come across our lives every day but many a time we do not cherish them we do not even recognize them.

Gratitude is the key to peace of mind and once you have peace of mind, you can work towards any goal, no matter how hard it is. The basic issue is that when we talk about two things i.e. comfort and monetary earnings we do not differentiate between our needs and wants. When you focus just on your needs, it is much easier to follow your passions and strive for even larger goals. The world is conspiring to make our lives simpler. But the mist of those material wants obscures our thinking process and perspectives. Therefore gratitude is the first step towards our well-being and peace of mind.

I mean how cool is it, that while you are feeling hungry, you can order your favorite food online through an app. It comes to you within 20 minutes. Also, the delivery boy makes you feel quite worthy by calling you "sir" and in case you tell him that you will give him full ratings, then that spark in his eyes makes your entire day. Similarly, you go to the movie theatre. You watch a 3D movie. And man that's an amazing experience! A different life lived in just 2 hours for some 200 bucks. Similarly, if you can overcome your desire of getting a better car than your neighbors or relatives, life is so cool. Just drive a small car; save money and with that goes on a trip and see the other aspects of the world. Again the issue is, that society has not achieved that level of maturity. No matter how much we deny the fact, what the neighbors will say or what the friends will say etc, bother us a lot. It may be at a different level of consciousness but it is always there. And the problem starts from here only. This problem is created by us and only us and it has to be ended by us. Therefore, small pieces of happiness can be found almost everywhere, we just need a broader mindset and of course the power of gratitude.

Sara Teasdale beautifully writes in her poem called " Barter" :

> Life has loveliness to sell,
> All beautiful and splendid things,
> Blue waves whitened on a cliff,
> Soaring fire that sways and sings,

And children's faces looking up
Holding wonder like a cup.
Life has loveliness to sell,
Music like a curve of gold,
Scent of pine trees in the rain,
Eyes that love you, arms that hold,
And for your spirit's still delight,
Holy thoughts that star the night.
Spend all you have for loveliness,
Buy it and never count the cost;
For one white singing hour of peace
Count many a year of strife well lost,
And for a breath of ecstasy
Give all you have been, or could be."

While walking back I was recalling the words of that rickshaw puller. He had some limited needs and dreams but he had some real gratitude toward life. He loved eating chicken once in two weeks from a nearby chicken outlet and there was a unique spark in his eye when he looked at the nearby outlet from there. Moreover, I could notice his unique bond with a street dog. There is a lot to learn about life and gratitude from such humble people.

X

THE PHOTO FRAME AND MY YEARS OF STRUGGLE

As I was walking back, my mind was flooded with the events of the day; with the words of rikshaw puller and also the questions of the panel. I went to my room and on the wall was hanging a frame of my favorite poem "IF" by Rudyard Kipling. For the last few years, I had read that poem almost every day and I had always believed that it is one of the best poems ever written on this planet. I just stood in front of it and read that poem once again. After that, I walked away and I tried to calm down my super active brain. I tried to play chess; tried to read the work of Rumi, but I wasn't able to concentrate. The questions of Lt. General Sir were popping up again and again in my mind. Whether I had answered rightly? Could I have added some more points? Oh! Did I miss that point? So, all this was running *in my mind.*

In the last few years whenever I had got overwhelmed with a flood of thoughts, I always used to do one thing: I would sit down to write a poem or I would do some random writing. That day I decided to write a commentary on the poem "IF" which had motivated me, guided me and supported me all these years.

Since ancient times, there have been numerous commentaries on major texts, for example, Patanjali's commentary on Panini's Ashtadyhayi; Shakaracharaya's commentary on Vedas, and so on. And once I began to write I spilled my last 10 years, while commenting on the lines of Mr. Kipling.

Horn of the train...

"I was in 8th class and it was the poetry recitation competition in my school. I had chosen the poem "IF". Before I recited my English teacher had explained to me the beautiful lines of this poem. But still, I didn't understand the real depth of those lines because it requires life experiences. And since last 5 years I had read this poem a million times or rather it will not be wrong to say that I had lived those few lines:

<u>If you can keep your head when all about you</u>
<u>Are losing theirs and blaming it on you,</u>

No matter how good you are. You will always find some people around you, usually playing the fake victims to justify their inner demons. The truth is that they are fighting unknown inner struggles. Hence the search for scapegoats. Even if you lack vices, they will themselves create one for you, to attack you or criticize you, because It soothes their inner wreck. They just cannot see anyone doing better than them or doing stuff that they could never risk doing.

Let us understand this more subtly. Some people have a kind of a crab mentality i.e. trying to pull others down. They are frustrated yoke, yet look normal to the society. They are the same people who once had some unique goals, but were absorbed by the average or sub-average life. And average life is not defined by the work you do, but whether what you do, is your actual interest or not? They had failed to gather enough courage to chase their unique goals, to take risks, to resist the endeavors of being absorbed and of course the intellect to understand the process of absorption itself. They have themselves messed up their lives and they live in a psychological conflict, every day, and every second of their lives by the virtue of their inherent contradiction, and yet they don't even know this. They are consistently in search of peace, maybe at an unconscious level. Therefore in the quest for that peace, they develop a kind of crab mentality i.e. to pull others down. And for that, there are several tools like over criticism, over opinionating, falsehood, downplaying, jealousy talks, etc. The world is a just see-saw for these people. By behaving like this, they think the other person goes down and they automatically rise. Moreover, it just requires the movement of the tongue and mouth, hence the process is much easier. Not only this, they would merely whisper about your good self or your unique virtues because talking about your virtues unconsciously reveals their own deficiencies. Moreover, they have a desperate zeal to find prestige in society and that too without doing anything to prove themselves or delve into the associated risks.

And yes definitely! They will never be true to their conscience. They will never accept the truth of their crab kind of behavior. If they accept their rascal being, it would further downsize their self-esteem. Interestingly, in the name of positivity, such people are very less talked about and as far as our dealings are concerned, the best way to deal with them is to just ignore these petty beings and move on. Arguing with them burns calories and moreover, as per thermodynamics, we should conserve our energies. Life is too short and the world is too huge, to focus on such people and we should focus on our job.

"If you can trust yourself when all men doubt you,
But make allowance for their doubting too";

Faith has enormous power and the human spirit is indomitable. Again it is much easier said than understood. Ambition, commitment and determination fuel the right attitude. And the source of all these three is self-belief. Attitude is nothing but the objectification of our values and convictions. It is the same driving force that made a water carrier become Balban the great; which made a simple soldier become Sher Shah Sur; which made a newspaper delivery boy become Dr. APJ Kalam. Moreover, the true difference comes in life when we become indifferent to the opinions of people. We cannot control the opinions of others, especially in India where you get opinions for free. And out of deep faith, one needs to keep working for one's goals.

Emily Dickinson writes

"Hope" is the thing with feathers -
That perches in the soul -
And sings the tune without the words -
And never stops - at all "

Let the other have opinions, let them have doubts. Have faith in the force of time and just ignore them, for the time will tell. It always tells! Therefore, no matter how difficult it is, one needs to become a silent bubble in the noisy ocean. Fidel Castro during his trial gave his famous quote,

"Condemn me! It doesn't matter. History will absolve me."

But in such quests, you need not start looking at success from their perspectives. It is very easy to get absorbed in those illusions. We need to stay true to our perspectives. It is possible that efforts may not yield results and then comes the role of "Nishkama Karma" i.e duty should become an end in itself. If there is something you love, something you think is worth striving for, then giving full efforts towards it becomes your duty. Moreover, full effort then becomes a full success. Even if you fail, then someday later in life or in your old age you will not regret having not tried or not giving your best. With your effort, you are eliminating future regret and regret is something, that makes life difficult.

An average mind is too immature to understand how a person can enjoy success without bearing the fruits. Only a person who has the courage to follow the path of "Nishkam Karma" can understand. This is the very path or the very force which is making "aspirants" wake up from their beds every morning and continue with their cyclic preparation even after four years of consecutive failures.

<u>"If you can wait and not be tired by waiting,</u>
<u>Or being lied about, don't deal in lies,"</u>

Waiting for the accomplishment of goals requires patience. The word is very often used by people. But its dimensions are huge. Patience means the power to delay instantaneous gratifications for something more meaningful. It means the power to accept contempt and lowering oneself and but definitely to that limit which doesn't violate your self-esteem. And alongside the intellect to differentiate the thin line between ego and self-esteem. (The latter becomes quite important in face of the "crab mentality people). Further, it means to never lose hope and to walk that crucial extra mile when you are exhausted. It means to never lose sight of the reason as to why you started.

Patience is not an autonomous value and true patience always complements the values like trust and self-confidence. Moreover, meaningful movies have always been close to my heart. I had an opportunity to see a 1994 film named Shawshank Redemption. The prisoner who has been falsely accused and given 2 life sentences, digs a tunnel for 20 years and that too with just one small hammer. Every day bit by bit, the person finally escapes to freedom. Therefore if there is something real to fight for, to quest for, then patience is extremely important. A few lines of poem invictus go like this :

In the fell clutch of circumstance

I have not winced nor cried aloud.

Under the bludgeonings of chance

My head is bloody but unbowed.

It matters not how strait the gate,

How charged with punishments the scroll,

I am the master of my fate,

I am the captain of my soul.

"Or being hated, don't give way to hating,

And yet don't look too good, nor talk too wise:"

A question arises that is there any person in this world who is not hated? Any single example? Mahatma Gandhi or some incumbent PM in some nation? A famous actor or some eminent and ethical journalist? There are 7 billion people, there are 7 billion perspectives. One's way of life may differ from others, one's values may differ from others. Just like there are numerous varieties of falsehoods, there are numerous truths in this world too. Mahavira calls this idea as "Anekantavada". The issue is not of difference but of lack of tolerance or the silly tendencies as discussed earlier, which makes some people hate others. Probably that is the reason that a person preoccupied with a negative mindset, tends to find vices, with the help of magnifying glass, even in the wisest person around and hence makes those vices as an excuse to hate a person. But again not every society is as progressive as the Japanese society and then few stanzas of Maya Angelou's poem go like this

> You may write me down in history
> With your bitter, twisted lies,
> You may tread me in the very dirt
> But still, like dust, I'll rise.
> Just like moons and like suns,
> With the certainty of tides,
> Just like hopes springing high,
> Still I'll rise
> You may shoot me with your words,
> You may cut me with your eyes,
> You may kill me with your hatefulness,
> But still, like air, I'll rise.

Similarly one should neither talk too wise. Life becomes difficult when you talk about a La La land or a Utopian world (talked by some socialists). Because ultimately our existence in society is with people, and those people are not accustomed to ultra wise methods of living. But that again doesn't mean that idealism has no relevance. Progressive changes in society are brought with hypotheses and theorizing. Idealism is a hypothetical construct that is difficult to achieve, as realities of life tend to continuously shift the equilibrium between the professed ideal and the present realities. But with idealism, one has better tools to escape the narrow enslaving impulses of life. Idealism is a tool that liberates us many times and prevents our entrapment.

<u>"If you can dream—and not make dreams your master;</u>
<u>If you can think—and not make thoughts your aim;"</u>

One needs to strive for one's dreams. But before that one should dare to dream. The demise of a man or a society starts when one doesn't dream or set goals in life. L. Hughes writes a poem

" Hold fast to dreams
For if dreams die
Life is a broken-winged bird
That cannot fly.
Hold fast to dreams
For when dreams go
Life is a barren field
Frozen with snow."

But as said earlier, it is possible that even after giving everything, and after putting in every possible effort, one may not be able to achieve the final milestone. If we let dreams become our master, we may actually be equating our dream to that of our whole life. In other words, we are equating dreams with our life. No matter how important your dream is one should never forget that one has taken birth at the peak of 4 billion-year-old human civilization. Life is extremely worthy as compared to any dream of the person, no matter how much value it holds. This world presents us with enormous opportunities to live our dream through different paths, different methods. It is just about giving your best and taking out the best, from yourself. Douglas Malloch writes

"If you can't be a pine on the top of the hill,
Be a scrub in the valley — but be
The best little scrub by the side of the rill;
Be a bush if you can't be a tree.

If you can't be a bush be a bit of the grass,
And some highway happier make;
If you can't be a muskie then just be a bass —
But the liveliest bass in the lake!
We can't all be captains, we've got to be crew,
There's something for all of us here,
There's big work to do, and there's lesser to do,
And the task you must do is near.
If you can't be a highway then just be a trail,
If you can't be the sun be a star;
It isn't by size that you win or you fail —
Be the best of whatever you are!"

If one path gets closed there is always another path to live the same dream and it is always fine to have a new dream, at any stage of your life. Life is all about the satisfaction of our preferences.

But the problem, to which I don't have any answer, is that if everyone follows this path of chasing their own dreams. How will this world function, how will societies progress? Once, my computer had broken down. A Technician came to my home. I asked him how was his job going. He said, "Sir company waalon ne buri haalat ki hui hai (The job pressure was too much)". I asked," Do you enjoy your job. He spoke after a small silence, "Sir bas chal rha hai. Khush to nahi hun (It's just going on, I am not happy though)." But the real thing! My laptop was repaired back. Maybe the answer is that it is good that some people are not/ cannot follow their dreams. Somehow, it is beneficial for those people who can.

> "If you can meet with Triumph and Disaster
> And treat those two impostors just the same"

Triumphs and disasters are part of life. Triumphs and disasters are all relative terms; relative in the context of both people and time.

Let us discuss the context of people first. Some, see triumphs only in the result, some see it in the effort to achieve those results. A failure may be an opportunity to learn for some and maybe an end of life for some narrow-minded people.

And as far as the aspect of time is concerned, sometimes a debacle turns out to be of huge benefit later in your life. Hence something which was once called debacle, later in life, becomes a god-sent opportunity for something much better. Then one realizes that what was once called failure, was not actually a failure. Hence the fantastic use of the word "impostor" by Mr. Rudyard Kipling. And the moment one realizes these simple, things, one is liberated from the fear of failure.

> "If you can bear to hear the truth you've spoken
> Twisted by knaves to make a trap for fools,"
> "Or watch the things you gave your life to, broken,
> And stoop and build 'em up with worn-out tools"
> "If you can make one heap of all your winnings
> And risk it on one turn of pitch-and-toss,
> And lose, and start again at your beginnings
> And never breathe a word about your loss"

These are some of my favorite lines in this poem. Desires enslave us. Effects of failure are enslaving many a time. But what one often forgets is that even our victories enslave us sometimes. Those victories are actually small. The fear that in the quest for a larger goal, one may lose, the benefits of hard-earned smaller goals, sometimes doesn't allow people, to risk for the higher aims. Hence one imposes self-incurred limitations on self, no matter how much potential one has.

Horn of the train........

It was the year 2010. I was getting a respectable engineering college in my city, but not the college I had aimed for. So I had decided to drop a year. Dropping 365 days of your life, for just 3 hours duration of the exam and that too with all the uncertainty, is quite difficult. The son of my aunt in the neighborhood had got a lower rank after dropping a year (as compared to his previous performance). The only difference when you appear after dropping is that pressure becomes huge, and that is quite natural. Given the warning, I took up the challenge and I had won it. Not by luck, but by some real hard efforts. I had secured seats, in the dream colleges of my parents, and from then onwards, first time in my life I had started striving for my dream, for a civil service job. An exam they call, one of the toughest exams in the world. Moreover, ignorant people claim as if the entire exam is about your luck; many of those who crack the exam, claim as if the luck factor is nearly zero. Lastly, some rational and sensible people claim that the luck factor amounts to around 30 % in this exam. Numerous factors like the corners from where preliminary questions are picked; the state of mind of the answer evaluators (across all the 7 mains exams); the interview panel which one gets etc, bring some luck factor into the exam.

Furthermore, the issue with the optional subject is that the best answers in humanities get to max 60-65% marks, while in subjects like Mathematics the best answer gets 100% marks. Therefore out of 500 marks, many Mathematics students touch 350 plus, while only a few touch 300 in the humanities. And moreover, my analysis of this exam has made me conclude, that there is no normalization amongst 23 optional subjects.

Also during the engineering exams, only potential engineering aspirants compete among each other. In this exam, the best minds from different fields compete amongst one another. In summation, hard work without any doubt, dominates a lot but the luck factor, does have an important role in this exam too.

After my engineering, there were two options before me. First, to take up the job, for which there was a lot of pressure on me, given the middle-class nature of my family. The second was to give full focus, towards my UPSC preparation. Further, rejecting a job is very difficult when you are almost being served a job on your dish plate, well knowing the fact that later if I take up the job, I may not get the same package or may be, finding a job would be quite difficult. Moreover, I was rejecting something, for which I had dropped a year in 2010; for which I had endured numerous difficulties that year. All this went through my mind, and I gave up the idea of job. The decision is easy for people from some well-off families, but not from a middle-class families.

I often cherish the words of poet Wasim Barelvi Sahab
"Sabhi ko shodhkar , khud par bharosa kar liya maine
Vo jo mujh me marne ko tha , zinda kar liya maine,
Safar mera kisi toofan ke dar se nahi rukta
Iraada kar liya toh bas kar liya maine"
After engineering, I preferred to stay at my home and give full focus towards the UPSC exam. But hardly had I known, what was in reserve for me. I had failed to crack the preliminary exam in 2015. But I improved and got through it in 2016 but couldn't qualify the mains exam. I then qualified for three more preliminary examinations of UPSC but every time I got stuck in my mains exam (and once just by 2.5 marks). Yes! Even those marks can cost you 1 whole year in UPSC. But the culmination took place in 2020 when I had squeezed the time for the preliminary exam,

thinking that I was clearing the exam for the last 4 times and I therefore, gave a greater focus on the Mains exam. The end of my UPSC journey took place with failure in preliminary examination by 1.1 MARK. I had secured 91.4 marks and the cutoff was 92.5. Now let me tell you something, I am a person who doesn't lie to my own self. This time the way I had prepared for mains, I was sure that I would have cracked the mains. But destiny had something else for me. Following the end of my UPSC journey, there was a strange peace but yes some pain too. It took me nearly 15 days to get over the realities and then I came to know that my parents had made all the preparations to send me to Canada (an interesting story to be covered later in the chapter: "The Race")

Therefore, between 2015 and 2020, I had faced many knockdowns and that too consecutively, but every time I would start fresh, would improve myself from my beginnings, with a hope to attain my goal someday. And of course with a thought back in my mind that even if I fail, I will feel satisfied that I had given my best . All I had known were two things: First that I have to keep improving. Second, that I will fight till the very end.

"If you can force your heart and nerve and sinew
To serve your turn long after they are gone,
And so hold on when there is nothing in you
Except for the Will which says to them: 'Hold on!'"

This is quite relevant to the story of aspirants. All I can say is that just imagine, sitting in front of your book for one month, in your room, 12 hours a day with little escapes like an evening walk. The load that you bear on your mind, just multiply that with 5-7 years (my case). One may then imagine, that with what kind of motivation, aspirants hold on with their struggle. There are examples in Rajinder

Nagar, of some candidates who are living there for the last 6 years and have gone to their homes just once or twice every year. Moreover, with every failed attempt, the baggage one carries into the exam hall increases.

It is just impossible to describe the no. of times I had pushed myself forth when I didn't feel like, because there are some limitations of the body's appetite too. But again it is always about bouncing back. While for the associated experience you may refer to the upcoming chapter: "The Race", I will like to make a mention of the few stanzas of Douglas Malloch's poem, the Good timber:

"Good timber does not grow with ease,
The stronger wind, the stronger trees,
The further sky, the greater length,
The more the storm, the more the strength.
By sun and cold, by rain and snow,
In trees and men good timbers grow.
Where thickest lies the forest growth
We find the patriarchs of both.
And they hold counsel with the stars
Whose broken branches show the scars
Of many winds and much of strife.
This is the common law of life"
"If you can talk with crowds and keep your virtue,
Or walk with Kings—nor lose the common touch"
"If neither foes nor loving friends can hurt you,
If all men count with you, but none too much"

Success spoils the mind of many, so you must uphold your humility. Moreover, in these lines Mr. Kipling has by default accepted that even the wisest person will have his/her foes. In my experience, I feel that in the first place, a person should have the ability to digest contempt and should work on enhancing one's patience levels and search for the real line between ego and self-respect. Thirdly, when it comes to your self-esteem and your principles, one needs to be face to face with petty idiots and throw them out of your life

Further, one needs to be helpful and trustworthy. These are the basic virtues of society. But the problem why people should not be counted upon too much is that helping and supporting beyond a limit, reduces the time and space for one's own efforts, for one's own goals. Come hell or high water, a person will ultimately become bad, by refusing to support beyond a limit. People do not remember the million times we helped them, rather they will remember the one instance when we say no. Moreover one shouldn't expect much from anybody. Expectations do hurt and as they say that not everyone in this world has the same heart as you.

<u>"If you can fill the unforgiving minute</u>
<u>With sixty seconds' worth of distance run"</u>

Mr. Kipling talks about the crucial moments in life. In these moments one has to do everything one can. These moments are the golden opportunities when one can push oneself up. For me, those moments were those 3 hours, in which I wrote the exam backed with an effort of many years. Those 3 hours have to be lived like never before. These are the unforgiving times. One small mistake can push you a year back. These moments require your mind, body, heart and soul, all working towards the same goal. All senses should be focused. The failure in doing so cost me a lot in 2015 and 2020.

<u>"Yours is the Earth and everything that's in it,</u>
<u>And—which is more—you'll be a Man, my son!"</u>

XI

SILENCE PLEASE!

After writing a commentary on the poem "IF" I secured something called a relaxed mind. Random writing and poem writing had always helped me in this way. So I just lay on my bean bag in silence and I felt the much-needed silence in my mind. The silence was not new to me, neither its form nor any of its dimension. For the last 7 years, I had stayed away from social media, I had a limited circle with whom I communicated. Lying on that bean bag was quite similar to the last 7 years of struggle.

Horn of the train..

In my childhood, I was once watching the film Rang De Basanti. There is dialogue towards the end, "Sometimes a person can push himself so far, to a place where there is a strange peace, where he is free to do the right thing and sometimes......that's the hardest thing to do". I hardly understood anything about these words. But now I do!

As far as my experience and experience of other aspirants are concerned, there is one observation (which might be valid for others too) that usually there are three categories of people around us.

First, who gives us advice, just because they are free enough to talk almost everything except sense! Second, the genuine well-wishers, who out of deep concern, render their advice to us. But there is an issue with both these categories. These people give advice, as per the limitations of their knowledge. In my experience, all advice during my preparation phase had one common presumption that one has to earn better for a good life. Hence the advice like, this job gives this much, the comfort level is this much. This is the very process that absorbs many people while they are in their twenties. This process sometimes also kills the unique aspirations of millions. It is a silent process of the homogenization of our society, a process of absorption of tender aged people, into the society which presents nothing more than some "above average or even shortsighted goals". There is a constant noise of advice all around us. Moreover, there is a very good element in Indian culture i.e. respecting the elders. But the issue is once you touch their feet; sometimes you unconsciously accept them to be much wiser. We are taught since childhood that elders are wiser. It's not like that. Sometimes, one of the biggest fools and idiots around us might be double or triple our age. Following them in the name of respect to the elders is not correct. I was once listening to Osho. He said, "Society doesn't want us to become wise". His simple logic is that society invests a lot in us. Parents may invest so that child earns better for them. The most brilliant students in schools are advised since childhood to join IIM, IIT, etc. A student easily gets influenced by the teacher. Tender age is just like that only but the child fails to realize his/her true dreams lying deep within. The noise around us suppresses the voice of our inner hearts. Even if the adolescent listens to that voice, then he/she many a time fails to put it strongly in front of the parents, in front of the so-called "wiser" uncles or relatives. Later one realizes that these people are captives of a small mindset of this materialistic world. And then they also think as is their duty to create replicas similar to them in this world. Therefore... noise follows!

Then comes the third category, ones with the crab mentality which we had already discussed.

There is the fourth category also, the rarest of the rare, ones who dare to chase their dreams. In fact, throughout my struggle, I came across just 5 such people. And whenever you come across them, just remain closer to them and that's what I did. For 9 months (January to September) I used to be in almost academic seclusion, away from the 3 categories of people. But I did keep myself close to these 5 people. They were the ones who were experiencing the same struggles, same difficulties as that of mine, and could give me some real advice and support.

Therefore, in a nutshell, silence and distance sometimes become very important. In today's world silence and seclusion are not accepted well but sometimes, they are extremely important as they untie you from the strings of some narrow-minded people. It gives you peace of mind and to do what you like; to introspect and improve. But if for the sake of something you believe in, when you distance yourself from others, make sure that you self-evaluate and do constructive criticism of yourself. But here is a caution, whenever you need help you have to reach out, you can't impose silence and seclusion upon yourself in an orthodox fashion. But yes! I am quite astonished as to how silence is seen as a negative thing in our society. Silence cannot be a way of our lives (for some ascetics it may be) but it should be a part of our life, especially during our struggles. Silence facilitates you to stay away from the unnecessary noise and it facilitates you to pursue your unique dreams.

And not only for aspirants even for other people, but Life can also take you on a busy ride such that you may often fail to realize its true purpose. One doesn't even have the time to think about whether the job satisfies him/her? Is this job his real passion? Life is so complicated that people avoid posing these questions to themselves, in order to avoid the inherent contradictions. Once a person gets absorbed into the work he doesn't like, then it is difficult to escape. Responsibilities further add up later in life. You start working for promotions, for decent salaries. Life gets compartmentalized on a small piece of land on this planet. On this patch, you are free and yet still not free. The chains are invisible and these chains were once your own choice. Sometimes one starts thinking later in life that if he/she had gathered a little more courage to walk that extra mile, things would have been different. This regret, that one should have tried a little more, kills oneself, every minute and every second in later part of life. Therefore to avoid that regret, Silence accompanied by frequent self-introspection and subsequently, the courage to act becomes extremely important.

Moreover, it is too idealistic to follow "suno sab ki , karo man ki (listen to all but follow your mind)". All the saints say that but we are humans, we get influenced. This mantra should be followed in general life and not at extreme moments of our struggle. The struggle already takes a huge toll of on one's brain. One cannot afford to spare extra energy to filter the useless opinions. Hence silence becomes important. Also as Dr. Amartya Sen claims in his book, the "Argumentative Indian", that Indians are argumentative by nature and we don't appreciate the value of silence fully.

Therefore after completing my college in 2015, and especially after 2017, I had preferred a silent mode, a seclusion mode where I was in touch with no more than 5-6 people beyond my family and neighborhood. I still witness many aspirants following it and I think it is the best thing they can do.

But there are some cautions associated with this silent phase. One who delves into deep silence is already a rebel. The mind becomes even more fertile for some greater possibilities of radicalism. True success of any person in this world lies in disciplining one's emotions, one's inherent conflicts. Therefore one has to be careful and moreover strength of adhering to truth and persistence of character, are always required for true glories in the life.

XII

THE RACE : UNTO THE LAST!

After 15 days of my interview, I had to visit Patiala once again. This time to qualify for the DSP physical test. In other states like Haryana, just height and chest measurement is sufficient but in Punjab, there are 5 requirements

- Maximum age limit of 28.
- Minimum Height and Chest requirements.
- 1600 meter race in 7.5 minutes.

And 2 of the following three

- High Jump: 3.75 meters
- Long Jump of around 12 feet.
- Rope climb 2 meters.

Until the test schedule came out, I was thinking that I will get 1 month to prepare, but all I got were 15 days. For the last 7 years, I had never done running or jogging. Though I had started the gym in January 2020 due to lockdown I had to stop it. A 30 minute evening walk was the only activity I did and the lockdown had made even that difficult.

So just from the next day of the interview, I started jogging, and from the third day onwards I had started running 600 meters in one go. Gradually the realities of training came in front of me. The cramps in my legs and ankles were quite painful, especially when for the last 7 years I had done no rigorous exercise. But somehow I was improving my stamina with every passing day.

Now I needed High jump and Long jump track but COVID restrictions had made that quite difficult. Somehow, I got the required permissions to practice in the sports complex sector 7, Chandigarh. It had a 400 meters well-maintained track, but strict guidelines of the institution restricted me from running on the track. So I shifted my practice to the police line sector 26, where I not only gained expertise in 2-meter rope climb but I also could practice running under some guidance.

Moreover, experts told me that cramps were quite natural and I had to deal with the pain. But one day, after I had run 1600 meters in the police line, I went to the sports complex for my long jump practice. All those who have done the long jump, know very well that the soil has to be plowed first, for a cushioned landing, otherwise injury might happen. I, on the other hand, having already exhausted myself after the race and out of a little over-ambition, attempted a long jump without plowing the landing strip. The jump was a total mess and I felt a strong pain in the lower part of my right knee but I thought it was a cramp. I knew I couldn't do the Long Jump, so I chose the High Jump instead out of the options list. But with every high jump attempt, the pain increased.

Moreover, I couldn't sleep because the pain would start in the middle of the night. I decided to see a physiotherapist well known for guiding Bhuvaneshwar Kumar. He asked me to stand in some positions and with some pity, he looked at me told me that I couldn't do the high jump or long jump as it would just worsen the tear. I made him clear that I will be appearing for the physical because it was a once-in-a-lifetime opportunity. He thought over a little and recommended ice baths, some expensive knee binders along some pain relief tablets.

I took a 2-day rest on his recommendation and it improved my situation but I noticed that I was losing time in the race as compared to my previous runs, so I experimented with different shoes; I bought gym equipment and tried my best but 15 days were way too less. We had to get a medical test done from a hospital to get clearance for the race and we had to sign a form, acknowledging that we were opting for the physical test at our own risk.

I had left all the training 2 days before the physical test so as to avoid any further injury. My mother had requested me to accompany me but I refused because she had already seen me in a lot of pain for the last 15 days. Therefore I went to Patiala a day before with Harwinder ji. Our test was to be conducted at Polo Ground Patiala. We went to the ground a day before and it was a very well-maintained 400 meters track. So as part of the strategy, I had divided one lap into 4 parts by remembering some key features of that track and I was all ready for the race.

We were to report at 5:00 AM and we were staying in the same hotel (Hotel Godwin), in which I used to stay during my mains exam. I took a light dinner and went to sleep but I didn't have a sound sleep as I was feeling a little anxious. I had trained myself for relaxing before my usual exams but this was something new.

At 5:00 we reached the stadium and Punjab police had sealed the entire road outside the stadium. We couldn't understand what was happening. Harwinder ji enquired from somebody and he told that race would take place on the road outside the stadium. We looked at each other and then we started laughing.

All the candidates stood on the starting line, no social distancing, no fear of corona just one the target i.e. to finish the race. The race began and I started with all my energy. My target was to remain in the middle of the running candidates. But gradually I realized that there was some real difference between running on the round track and on the road as there were no markings. On a track, you can analyze how much you have run and how much distance is remaining and that automatically motivates you. But here due to pain and breathlessness, I started losing my rhythm. Though I was still ahead of many candidates I was losing on time.

I was nearly 50 meters away from the finish line and I realized that the race was over. Few candidates were lying on road just behind the finish line, as they had also failed to finish the race. I stopped at that dismal sight and I looked to my right and there was a swarm of parents standing with a pin drop silence or maybe my eardrums were numb. Then I looked back, a candidate had collapsed on the road and a policeman was offering him a bottle of water. And while standing there, I was feeling pain, I was feeling breathlessness, and I too wanted to collapse then and there on the road.

And then,

Horn of the train..

In October 2020, my mother delivered the news that I couldn't clear my last preliminary and I had exhausted all my UPSC attempts. 9 years, 2 months and 28 days back I had started my UPSC preparation. I had fallen from the cliff when the top was near, very near and I saw tears in her eyes but I was beyond any pain. That kind of pain had stopped affecting my mind, for long. So in peace, in silence, I took out the photo of my grandfather (always in my drawer of my study table) and said sorry to him. I knew, I did all I could. He knew, "I did all I could". My parents were apologizing to me for some reason and I said, "Why? It was my dream, it was my passion". Mom said," For not for having the courage to push you out of this crazy struggle." I laughed and said, "Don't joke please!"

Mom was not amazed to look at my calm and composed behavior. She was accustomed to seeing this after each of my UPSC knockdowns. After the end of my UPSC journey, there was a lot of pressure on me to go abroad. My parents had even talked to my uncle and aunt residing there and had made all the arrangements. They tried to convince me for one entire week, but I refused. PCS exam was near and a PCS officer is also a bureaucrat, what if had lost my dream to become an IAS officer and of serving in the northeast. As a PCS officer, I could get a promotion as an IAS officer and all was not over yet!

David Beck has proven that what others will think of you, restricts your risk-taking capability and of experimenting with something new.

Unfortunately, we as a society are not mature enough to appreciate the innate values of others. We are just groomed to see the material achievements. But I must say that a person rebelling the society while working on his ideals, a person treading the path of unconventionality, a person trying to test one's limits; a person trying to do something never heard before; a person who can live and work on his dreams in silence amidst all the addictive noise; a person who lives with the idea of " Nishkam Karma" is a man of some real substance and this notion is quite poorly recognized in our society. There are some glories, that are real, which are silent, which are substantive, and that makes our life worth living. Moreover, Y. Harari says, "99% people in the world are roaming out with a virtual tag on their head stating, "Make me feel important." And our mind is trained to think about heuristic shortcuts in that direction and when we don't get appreciation we feel demotivated. That is a challenge that aspirants face.

Moreover, Osho once said, "The only life worth living involves risks, adventure, some real unconventionality, some challenge to the norms". Moreover, attachment with the results - "was, is and shall" always be an inhibitor of the individual initiatives. I believe that ideas that appreciate people for their initiatives, unique passions, and their efforts (and not the results), are the ideas that belong to the future, but yes! Not far future.

And therefore, I had no option but to still believe in myself and I started convincing my parents for one last chance. They on other hand pointed out the tough odds in the PCS exam. If the success rate in UPSC was 0.0015. It was just 0.00028 in Punjab Civil service exam because I was competing for just 16 seats in the state of Punjab. Moreover, I had not been in touch with the Punjabi language for long. In my final word, I told my mother to look at my academic record, I had always finished, what I had started and she knew that very well."

And there I stood 50 meters behind the finish line, knowing very well that 10 minutes before I was competing for 16 seats of P.C.S. exam, and now with the race over, I was competing for just 9 seats. I was out of the race for D.S.P. seats. I was standing there with fallen candidates both in front of me and behind me and I had nothing left in me, but still, I began to run towards the finish line and somebody in the group of parents shouted, "Shaabash beta! (well-done son!)". I somehow reached the finish line and I collapsed there. Harwinder ji told about the race to my parents and with a slight hope amongst the 9 remaining seats, we left Patiala. The results were to be announced in the next 2 days.

XIII

THE RESULT: WHEN THE TIME STOPPED!

UPSC had taught me to deal with the anxiety of the result. It was 18th June, the last day of the interview and I was sure that the result would be declared on the same day. I had spent time in the morning: reading the poems, playing chess, staring at my books in the cupboard, watching the street dog Lucy(I had rescued her from the net of municipal corporation dog catchers as people were sick of her aggressive nature, an act which fetched me the wrath of some of the neighbors as well as my parents).

Subsequently, I took lunch and went to bed for an afternoon nap. Just as I woke up, I opened up the PPSC website, and the result was there. For an aspirant, this is the most nerve-wracking moment but thanks to my sleep, my overthinking senses were temporarily dead. I opened the combined merit list. My name didn't appear in the top 10.

I moved forward, and I found my name at the 17th Rank. It was an amazing rank. I had secured one of the highest marks in the interview but I was confused that in the context of the posts, whether it was all over for me or not. The reason was that, in the combined merit list, 5 candidates from reserved categories were ahead of me and my rank in the general category was 12.

I told the Rank to my mother, she hugged me, but like me, she was also confused in the context of the post allocation. Hence it was not a sudden "yay" moment for us. The hunt for information began, whether reserved category candidates can enter a general category, and we also looked for some more facts. By evening we had found the following facts:

- Out of 6 reserved candidates, only 1 could enter the general category
- That a candidate with Rank 11 (general) was selected as DSP and hence 1 seat was cleared for me.
- That a person with Rank 10(general) was already a Tehsildar and was not getting an SDM post. Hence another seat was cleared.
- That women reservation is horizontal, and therefore, already there were more than 33% girls above my rank, hence women candidates with lesser ranks couldn't surpass me in posts.

The conclusion was: "I HAD GOT THROUGH" , and I was getting the last seat (As per the perception then) in the general category of PCS exam 2020. Celebrations broke out in the home. I had made it through one of the toughest state civil service exams in India. 9 Years and 11 months of effort had brought the result. I had shown some reckless patience and reckless perseverance. The feelings on the day of 18th June 2021 were unimaginable. Those who had seen the results were calling me en masse. The no. of calls I received that day were probably the sum no. of calls I had received in the last 5 years

I had stayed away from social media for the last 7 years. I wanted to burst out on Facebook. But somehow I controlled my emotions. The following day, I received some information regarding category conversions into the general category, which again pushed me into a little uncertainty. But I was still confident because three candidates in the top 8 ranks in the general category, were yet to appear in the USPC interview. So if they would have gotten through in the UPSC exam, more seats were yet to be vacated. But like some other PCS rankers, I decided to wait till the UPSC result, before I could break the information to everyone. Meanwhile, people who knew my Rank were sure that I would get a post, so I stayed relaxed in the waiting period and headed towards the mountains again.

XIV

BHAGSU WATERFALLS AND THE FLUID DYNAMICS

USPC results were still awaited and in July, I decided to go on a trip to Chail, Thanedar, and Narkanda. The mountains serve as a balm on city roasted souls and on similar lines, Himachal had always been a huge relief for me. I went there with my cousin who had seen my hard work in the last 10 years quite closely. I always loved traveling to the mountains because you understand how small you are. For example, if you are traveling on the roads of Theog and Fagu and the tire of your bus is just a few inches away from a thousand feet deep valley, and you with no control over the steering, are just sitting there and watching this from the bus window, then no matter who you are or what you have achieved, you will appreciate your mere existence on this planet and a sense of gratitude automatically increases in you.

Moreover, it was my first monsoon in the mountains and the views were awesome, especially in Chail. In Chail, I had an opportunity to visit the heritage Gurudwara managed by a cheerful old person Pritpal Singh. He had done a master's in Punjabi from PU. Single-handedly he had maintained and upgraded the Gurudwara complex. As a man in his late 70s, he runs a Facebook page to mobilize funds from NRI and he was the one who had brought electricity back into the Gurudwara complex when the connection was cut for many weeks in the year 2013. Not only this, he gets excited when he sees the visitors as the Gurudwara is a little less visited, and he acts as their guide and tells them the history of Gurudwara. He can be seen clicking selfies with the visitors for his Facebook page. The good thing about meeting such people is that you understand your nothingness in front of such great yet humble people.

I came back afresh like always but of course this time with a little less tension. Counseling was to take place in December and UPSC results were still awaited. Meanwhile, in September, I went to the Triund Trek. It was my second Himachal visit in 3 months and what I was doing was a rebound from the 2020 lockdown (a worldwide phenomenon called "revenge tourism" by W.T.O.). I had booked a package with a hospitality company and I was ready for my second trek to the Triund top.

But a unique experience was awaiting me. There are two trails to the Triund top, one through Bhagsu waterfall which is steep and more dangerous, and the other through

Gallu temple which is a moderate yet longer trek (of nearly 7 km). The tourist guide took me through the Bhagsu waterfall route, where a cloudburst had taken place earlier this year. At the beginning of the trek, a policewoman stopped the guide and he took her away and they were talking about something. The policewoman didn't agree on something and a suspicion emerged in me. I asked about the matter but he didn't disclose so he took me through an alternate route from a small nearby village. It felt as if he was taking a small diversion on the same Bhagsu route, to surpass that police checkpoint, but I wasn't sure, and neither I had known, why? It was a famous company which I thought, wouldn't violate govt. rules but still I became a little vigilant.

We walked across the steep trail and then we came to a point where we reached the top of the Bhagsu waterfall. The bottom of the waterfall is a tourist destination but the top is very less visited. It was a picturesque and amazing scene. The fast-flowing water was falling several feet down on the rocks, from where Bhagsu rivulet further flowed deep down over a steep mountain. Moreover, the waterfall becomes a little ferocious during the monsoons and that was quite visible.

I appreciated the beautiful scene and told my guide with a smile as to how fast the water was flowing. He smiled back and said one of the most spectacular words I had ever heard in my entire life, "Sir! Please remove the shoes and fold up your pants. We have to cross the waterfall and reach the other side".

Dead silence prevailed between us. I looked at him and he

looked at me. The smile of that idiot creature was just like the smile of a Cheshire cat which was just not going off. Then I looked at the velocity of the water. I swear to god that in the last 9 years I had never recalled the concepts of fluid dynamics. But somehow with god's grace, I calculated the flow rate of that damn flowing water and I replied to him gently, "I will definitely remove the shoe bro, but I will hit you with them. So, do you want me to remove?" He said, "Arre sir! We cross this every day" and I said, "I can also tell you with surety that every year at least 1 person dies while crossing this furious water during the monsoons." He lowered his eyes, paused, and said, "Sir! Why think negatively!"

Amidst, my talking with this stupid creature, I got some déjà vu and now I understood why that policewoman was guarding this route. This route was banned by the H.P. government. So then, I called the company office straight away and threatened them with legal action not only via e consumer complaint in the consumer court but also with the H.P. Police. The person melted straight away and sought an apology. I shamed him in front of that guide, as they were openly threatening the lives of tourists. The water was almost at the knee level and if you slip, you fall feet below on the huge boulders and after that, hundreds of feet further deep down into the valley. I had already used the metaphor of falling from the hills in my poems but I didn't want that to become a reality. The person then talked with a guide and asked him to get me back. He then texted me on Whatsapp, that it will not happen again and the fee shall be refunded. But I was amazed at those strange and unethical people.

Subsequently, I came down to Mcleodganj. While parting away from that guide, I knew that his name was definitely not what he was telling me and I asked him strictly, "Should I take your pic and report it to the police on Mcleodganj square." "Nahi sir", he replied. Then I asked him frankly, "Do people die there every year?" He said, "Haanji sir! Last year a Bengali and his friend died while crossing that waterfall but they were just unlucky that day". I said, "They were not unlucky bro, they were careless and you people misguide them and risk the lives of tourists for the sake of money". Looking at his face, all I could do is, I made him swear on his local god that he will not repeat it, though only God knows if he will mend his ways or not.

The day was an utter mess and so I decided to extend my trip by one day. Police officials were standing on the Mcleodganj square. I asked them if that Bhagsu route is banned. They said, "Yes". I asked how come the guides are still violating the rules. They said many guides were from nearby hamlets, and hence they were aware of the alternate diversions and hence were difficult to control. I suggested the police officer to put a big banner near the Bhagsu temple as the trekkers go through that temple only, and hence the tourists could be informed about the government ban as well as the associated danger. They agreed. They also revealed that every year tourists die while crossing that waterfall and that last year the bodies of Bengali friends were found by local Gaddi goat herders deep down in the valley. Ridiculous it was!

I then stayed in McleodGanj that night. It was nowhere as crowded as it was before the Corona times. The hotel workers were standing on roads and were offering discounts to the tourists, on the room fares. One could notice the kind of a mess, the crisis from Wuhan had brought. Moreover, on the Mcleodganj square, two chicken shops were facing each other with a common passage. As I walked through that passage, the workers in the two shops came near me and simultaneously asked me to visit their shops, which turned the moment a little awkward. Similarly, many shops were closed and it was a different McleodGanj than the one I had seen in 2017. After dinner, I was loitering around and I came across a "Theka (alcohol shop)" which was crowded as usual. Throughout my life, I had never consumed alcohol. That day I had decided that I will consume a beer. I went to the shop and asked for the mildest beer. I brought it to my hotel room and took the first sip. It tasted like hell, but definitely, it was quite mild and facilitated a good night's sleep which I often find difficult on the hotel beds.

The next day I decided that I will try the Gallu temple route to the Triund top. I walked from Mcleodganj to Gallu temple on foot and there I visited the police check post and found that the route was legally open for tourists and it was the second day of its opening. For the last couple of years, I had always cherished, walking alone on the treks. When I came last time on the Triund trek, I was told that the area is infested with bears but I had confirmed that it happens in peak winters only. So I started my trek and after 30 minutes, I found myself in a different world, a beautiful world where I was all alone. No sign of humans or the creed of humans. It was just me and the mountains. I made a video call to my mother and showed her the scenery. She knew about the Bhagsu incident so instead of enjoying it, she started acting like an Indian mother, and I had to regret my decision to call.

Unlike 2017 when the trek was crowded and noisy, it was lying in its pristine form, and coupled with the overcast monsoon clouds I just loved the scenery. It was nothing less than bliss. Some places on the trail did make me a little nervous but that was a part of the overall thrill. The good thing about this trek is that whenever you get confused about the right direction there are markings that show you the right way. Therefore it is a safe route.

Earlier in 2017, there used to be 5 food stations on this 7 km trek, but now there was just one called the Moonlight café and the owner was quite friendly. He told me some interesting stories as to how some drunken trekkers had to be dragged from the nearby places and he had to shelter them. Once a drunk guide fell into a fight with tourists and he jumped deep down into the valley. His stories were as interesting as his style of cooking Maggi. And after that, I moved further and in the later phase it became a little steep and I had to stop more often to collect my breath. And by noon I was on the Triund top. I just cannot describe the view in words. I kept sitting and observing and suddenly I recalled my promise to a fellow traveler. I had met her at the Dharamkot square, as she was going for the famous Vipassana meditation course. She had requested me to send the pictures, as soon as I see the first view of Triund top.

The forest house was closed for tourists and I hired a private accommodation for 1 night. With a cup of coffee, I sat on the balcony, enjoying the view; looking at Mcelodganj (from where I had started that day), and now the whole city was fitting into my finger ring. That's how you come to know how small you are on this planet.

While sitting there I heard a language that was typical to my father's Majha region of Punjab. The two boys were from Gurdaspur region and we became good friends. We decided to trek even further to a place called Lahesh caves. So after roaming around there for a while, we left for the trek and in just 15 minutes I understood that it was a different creed of a trek, and some points were as steep as 70 degrees. The mist had accompanied me for the entire Triund trek but now it was quite foggy and the trail was not visible, even at a distance of a few meters. The directions were not well marked and I decided to walk back. The two of them tried to convince me a lot but I requested them to go there without me. Moreover, earlier that year, the "black ice" region of Kheerganga trek had taught me some real lessons. Finally, the two of them were in some confusion too, but they had decided to move forward.

Meanwhile, I came down on Triund top and was reading the poetry of Ahmad Faraz. Suddenly after 20 minutes or so, I heard a voice from behind," Bhaaji (bro), you were right about the trail, beyond that it is even more dangerous and we too decided to come back". We laughed I was in some really good company. The night on the Triund top was even more awesome. We played Punjabi songs; we danced and also made the property owner dance with us. Nearby, a sleepy dog was still sleeping amidst the loud music.

That night McleodGanj looked nothing more than 10 distant lamp posts. Sitting there I asked the Gurdaspur guys if they worked. One of them replied, "If we had jobs here in Punjab, why would we go to Canada?" Actually, both of them were going to Canada the following month and had come to enjoy the sceneries of Himachal for one last time.

The following day we trekked down together and I paid them my farewell at the Gallu temple. That trek had induced a new interest in me i.e. to visit Himachal during monsoons.

XV
TRYST WITH SOCIAL MEDIA

The UPSC results came in September and two of the three PCS candidates made it to I.A.S. and I.P.S. And the one selected for IPS was my college junior, a very talented and welfare-oriented person (already a Tehsildar), a good friend of mine, and who used to work with me in the Rotary club of my college. It was clear that I would get the post of Labour welfare and Conciliation officer and in fact, two candidates with ranks below me had also got through.

Now it was the time to post about my rank on Facebook. A lot of people were unaware of my rank in PCS for the last 3 months. Like many PCS rankers, I had preferred to wait till the UPSC results to update our profiles.

Horn of the train........

For the last 7 years, I had rarely used Facebook and now when I was going to post on Facebook, there was a new trend of Instagrams and Snapchat. My profile pic (the photo of Bhagat Singh and Che Guevara) was a decade old but I didn't feel like changing it. Social media had evolved a lot in the last 7 years.

Yuvah Harari refers to social media as the third most populous nation, just two decades old and which has no definite geographic boundaries. Moreover, connectivity and communicating form the basis of sharing, learning, debating and discussing. Social Media is not only changing how people communicate but also what people communicate. Social media is becoming an integral part of our life. Our day starts with checking and updating our social media accounts and it ends on a similar note.

But all these years, like many aspirants I had preferred to stay away from it. It has brought many revolutionary transformations in the world.

In politics, it had been used as a tool for political campaigning and advertising; as a tool for eliciting opinion of people on schemes, initiatives, and legislation; as a tool for policy implementation and monitoring; as a tool for enforcing transparency and accountability; as a tool for mobilizing support for a political movement, for example, the role of Social media in winning elections for Barack Obama; MyGov.in the portal by the Government of India for taking feedback from people, etc. Similarly, social media has given rise to citizen Journalism and it is now being touted as the 5th pillar of democracy. As far as the social dimension is concerned it has helped in making people more tolerant, aware of others' beliefs, culture, etc. Further, it has enabled people to maintain contact with families, friends, relatives, etc. It has aided in giving voice to voiceless people like Women, Black people in USA, Tribals, etc. Examples include #Metoo Campaign; #BlackLivesMatter etc. As far as the economic aspect is concerned, it is a new source of employment, as every organization now has a separate social media department. Further, it is a tool of feedback for companies. Similarly, e-Commerce has got a boost via social media; it has facilitated innovative start-ups and digital marketing and has even enabled remote handicrafts. Not only this social media has also enabled people to become more consciously aware of the environment and environmental protection for example the rise of the European Green Party (EGP) to a large extent is attributed to social media activism. In a nutshell, social media have emerged as a revolution in the 21st century.

But during my preparation phase, I had two reasons to remain away from it. First was the issue of FOMO (Fear of Missing Out). Continuous comparing our lives with others is mentally unhealthy; also social media is making it tough for people to engage in prolonged concentration. Moreover, studies have found that social media usage triggers more sadness and lesser well-being. The second was the problem of social media addiction. It is widely prevalent and as per one experiment, a working person uses his phone 112 times in a day and that too is predominantly because of social media. Moreover, studies have found that social media usage triggers more sadness and less well-being. These were not only my reasons but the reasons of majority of the aspirants who stay away from social media during preparation.

Apart from this, other issues include dopamine addiction. People (especially youth) try to present their "best selves" to the digital world (while the reality may be different), then they start identifying with those "fabricated digital selves". This is closely related to the commodification of life where every aspect of life is being open for public consumption, for example, the craze for selfies, location updates, etc. More "likes and comments" releases Dopamine in their brains and that makes them feel good. Moreover, before the digital era, people used to work hard in their lives to get that good feeling. But now via social media mode, it takes 2 minutes to achieve that. Though in a sense, that is also good, but sometimes people become over-dependent and they tend to become hollow in their real lives. For example when Tik Tok was banned, an astonishing no. of young people committed suicides, because they had attached their "whole existence" to a social media platform. Moving ahead, the second issue is the Carpal Tunnel Syndrome affecting hands or wrists because of too much typing. The third is a distraction, the most dangerous potential consequence of social media addiction is driving while being distracted by it. E.g. several road accidents are happening owing to the usage of mobiles. Fourthly, lack of exercise - social media is making people, especially children, lazy and immobile by cutting the duration, which they would otherwise be spending outdoors for exercising.

Therefore social media today has emerged as a double-edged sword. While it has transformed the way we think, believe, and act, it has led to numerous problems and therefore a "red line" needs to be identified beyond which one should not use social media.

And as far I am concerned, I had adhered to the "special red line" prescribed for aspirants and now it was the time to post. I posted and within 5 minutes, even before I could see likes and comments, I started receiving calls from near and dear ones and without doubt, it is an amazing experience for every aspirant.

XVI
THE CHALLENGER FRIEND

Now was the time of post allocation. Counseling took place exactly 6 months after the declaration of the result. It took place in MGSIPA sector 26, Chandigarh, a training institute for bureaucrats. The interesting thing was that all the 175 candidates were called for counseling, though just 75 posts were there. No doubt all of us were toppers and everyone deserved a post but it was a little weird to call 100 extra students and make them sit and watch, as to how close they were and yet so far.

I was sitting in the hall and suddenly I realized that a candidate was sitting just 3 seats next to me who had secured a Rank around 70-75 in that exam (but was not getting any post).

Horn of the train....

I was in class 4th and I had stood first in the class and the second ranker approached me. He challenged me that he would defeat me the next time but somehow he failed. Then in 5th class just before the exams, he again came to me and threw a similar challenge. But I stood first again, and the same repeated in the next two terminals. In the

6th class, he stopped throwing me challenges because now I was defeated by a newcomer and therefore we became good friends.

Unfortunately, he left my school in 7th class. Then came the time of the engineering entrance exam, I had failed to make it to IIT, BITS, and PEC in the first attempt but he made it to PEC University of Technology in the first attempt. And I had decided to drop and reappear for IIT, BITS, and AIEEE. During that dropping year, there was a Diwali "get together" of friends and he had also come. Now he was in the first year of mechanical engineering in PEC and I was still struggling. I still remember that he took me aside and said, "We had started the journey together and..... Now look!!!....." I kept quiet and laughed. I didn't mind because he was super competitive. The following year, I made into all three: IIT, BITS as well as PEC, and during my first visit to the PEC University, coincidently we met again. He showed me the entire college as well as the PEC market. And again a coincidence, I had also got admission in mechanical branch and I was now 1 year junior to him. But since he was struggling with his CGPA and he had some backlogs in the course of NSS, he had to do that course with me. Subsequently, he also didn't take placements from University and just like me, he dedicated his after college years towards civil service examinations. I used to see him here and there during the UPSC mains exam and we met once again in PCS preliminary exam 2018. He got through and reached the interview stage (though couldn't qualify), but I failed to pass the preliminary exam because I couldn't prepare well (my UPSC mains exams were approaching). After that, we met again during the interview preparation stage of this PCS exam 2020, in a zoom meeting of a coaching institution. He had noticed me sitting in the zoom meet but he didn't say anything. So during the break, I called him by his name and said, "Hello". He didn't respond and was smiling looking down. I said hello again and he somehow replied with a "Hi". That was my last memory of him."

And what a coincidence he was sitting just 2 seats next to me! But, if you were to ask me, deep down I was feeling sad for him. Getting ranked around the 70s is not a small thing. But as I said earlier also, "general male" candidates were competing for just 16 seats. He knew quite well that he wouldn't get any post but still he was there. Moreover, he had seen me sitting there while he was walking past me and he congratulated me. Sitting there, I wished he would have also got a post but I was quite sure that he will get through in UPSC or some other state exam in the future.

The counseling began and they started calling us rank-wise. Just before me, a crisis took place on the stage. A candidate from Bathinda and a good friend of mine were allocated the last SDM post in the general category. But after allocation, it was announced that his seat was canceled due to some issue of category conversion. His case was fair as he took the examination under his economically weaker section category but since he had surpassed the general cutoffs in all stages, he was eligible for a seat in the general category. God knows why they had confusion on this and once his seat was declared canceled, he had to go on the stage and explain his case. After 10-15 minutes it was clarified that he will be allotted the SDM post.

Sitting there, I was thinking that if I had got 3.5 marks more I would have got the executive post. But then I realized that I had got the only post of Labour welfare and conciliation officer in Punjab out of the 75 notified posts.

Horn of the train....

In 2014, as part of the Rotary club of my college PEC University of technology, I had created a project called Socio-economic empowerment of destitute, which I had presented in the Rotary district assembly so that rotary clubs from other regions of North India could adopt and implement the projects in their region. The following year, my project had won the best award in the entire North Indian Rotary district 3080, in the "Vocational training" category which was directly related to labour empowerment. Moreover, our work in Rotary was specifically oriented towards the empowerment of the weak and destitute. Similarly, we used to market the candles, made with the labour and sweat of handicapped people. Alongside I also worked for an NGO called Junior Einstein through which I used to teach children above 16, rehabilitated by another NGO, which was further working for their self-employment and skills."

And sitting in that counseling hall, I realized that I was being allocated the only Labour welfare and conciliation post. No matter, how much we deny the role of destiny, based on empiricism and science, sometimes it has a huge role to play in the direction of our lives.

My turn came. My name was called and it was quite a glorious moment to walk "DOWN" the stairs and then "UP" the stage.

Horn of the train.....

In February 2021, I was in Barshaini, a place near Kasol from where Kheerganga trek starts. I had to move "down" a steep hill before my climb began "up" to the Kheerganga top. I was moving down very slowly and was also struggling a bit and 3 students from IIT Roorkee (also trekking to Kheerganga) were observing this from behind. They were to accompany me for the entire journey and while on the trek, one of them was referring to that weird steep descent and as to how carefully I was moving down and I said, "A descent always precedes a glorious climb".

I walked up the stage, sat on the chair, and filled some forms. It was an emotional moment for me. 10 years before I had started my journey and now I was signing my allocation form. I was so submerged in my journey that I couldn't fill out the police form 2 times. The candidate appointed to the last SDM post was telling me about the mess he faced on the stage and I was just saying "Haanji Haanji" without listening. My journey was dancing in front of me. I later told my experience to another batch mate and he said he was shivering while filling out the form.

After the counseling, we roamed around the institute campus and a get-together of all the PCS officers was planned in a nearby restaurant. It was amazing to see the faces, which we had seen only on YouTube. There I came across an officer who had become SDM this year and earlier he was a Labour Welfare and conciliation officer. A very humble person as he was, though I had not asked for, he gave me his number for any guidance or query. Similarly, I came across two officers who belonged to the villages, quite near to the village of my mother in Muktsar Sahib. It was a jovial environment, and while sitting there, I was still not able to get over the thoughts of my 10-year long journey. And amidst all this, I got a call from Labour department of Punjab, and they requested me to get my documents verified in MGSIPA immediately, but I refused. I just didn't want to miss that moment.

From Chandigarh, unlike earlier times, only 2 candidates were selected for PCS, one was me, and the other was my coaching friend who got the last DSP post in the general category. Subsequently, we all got an opportunity to introduce ourselves, know each other and the pics of that get-together remain one of the most memorable moments of my life.

XVII

THE VILLAGE SCHOOL

It had been 6 years since I visited my mother's village Tarkhanwala in Muktsar Sahib. It was named so because this village was established by a zamindar Baba Mal Singh, during the reign of Farukhsiyar at the request of his very close friend who was a carpenter named Bhagwan Singh. And now the B.T. machines manufactured by people of this village are quite famous in Punjab. Similarly "Mata Rani da mela" in this village is also quite famous in the Malwa region.

I was traveling to my village with Maamaji (maternal uncle). I had brought a box of sweets for my maternal grandmother, the strongest lady I have ever known in my life. She had struggled a lot to rear my mother and Maamaji and hence she is respected a lot in the village. She had recently stood for Sarpanch elections but had lost by a close margin. Since childhood, I had always loved listening to the stories about her struggles. She usually sleeps by 8:00 PM.

But with me there, she wouldn't get tired of telling me the stories till midnight. And after a long talk, she requested me something, to go to the government school, where my grandfather used to teach and she asked me to deliver a lecture over there.

I agreed and requested my Maamaji to take me there. Once there first I met all the teachers of the school and then I visited the 10th class. Many teachers stood by me in the room and so did my Maamaji. My motivational speech went on for 20-30 minutes and there was pin-drop silence. As I left the room, Maamaji came to me and hugged me, and held me for quite some while. After that, he told me that he had put his phone on video call secretly and his mother was watching too back in Chandigarh. Then the teachers congratulated me for all the good words and I sought permission to roam around the school. The infrastructure was average but some parts of the school needed some up-gradation.

We came back and it was just the second night that I got a call from a senior Police official of the Punjab government. He told me that some officials will visit my home the next day for police verification. I was confused because my verification was already done by Chandigarh Police but then he said that it had also to be done by Punjab police. I told him that I was in my village in Muktsar and I needed a day to come back. He agreed and I had to cut short my village trip and go back.

The next day in the morning, he called back and asked me to reach the nearest Police thana i.e Sadar thana Malout within 15 minutes for physical verification while my document verification was already going on in my Chandigarh home simultaneously. While we were on the way, he asked me to change my route towards Muktsar city, as I had to reach the DSP office in Muktsar. We reached the office and I found that D.S.P. sir was very humble man. He also belonged to a village near Tarkhanwala. He apologized for the inconvenience and offered me tea. He was already in touch with Chandigarh officials and subsequently, he clicked my photo while drinking milk and my verification was therefore finally done. I don't know after how long I had visited Muktsar Sahib. Except for a few big hotels which had emerged, nothing had changed much. Though "Muktsari jutti"(shoes) was less visible but the popularity of white Kurta Pyjamas and that too with "Luppis" on shoulders, was the same as before.

Once back in my village, I visited a nearby house, where lived a lady to whom as a child I used to call "Bakri waali bibi" (an old woman who kept goats). She and her entire family were not in good socio-economic conditions. Originally they were migrants from U.P. but they had been living in the village for the last 60 years. Her daughter-in-law came to me and she touched my feet and I suddenly stopped her. Bibi, told me that it was a custom of their UP village. But a person who was missing in that house. As a kid, I used to play with her nephew, who was a good friend of mine, but now he was no more and had died 3 years ago because of drug addiction. Her son-in-law lived in Ganganagar and was an astrologist. My grandmother was in touch with him regarding the prospects of my "Sarkari Naukri (government job)", for the last 5 years and every time, he was like, "This time he will surely get through". Though, that's a different thing that his usual "this time" got quite delayed. While sitting there, Bakri waali bibi kept talking about his son-in-law's great predictions, and with a gentle smile, I kept listening and nodding.

After that my cousin, took me to the fields and I saw the signs of stubble burning ash and asked local farmers as to why don't use alternatives. They said it costs them Rs 5000 per acre more if they use alternatives like happy seeders etc. My village was still not aware of the new affordable innovations like Fungi bins, invented in Delhi.

XVIII
LOOKING BACK

There is a tendency of a lot of people to attach themselves to the outcomes of struggles. No doubt outcomes are important too. Let me be frank, I would not have been that happy if I had just secured a rank and would have not got a post. But the issue is that in modern society, the process and the struggle are outrightly ignored as if it was some useless endeavor; as if it was some waste of time; as if your failure to get an outcome amounts to wrecking yourself. Due to this very notion, I have seen numerous people around me, avoiding risks. While some of the aspirants I had known had some genuine reasons to leave the preparation after a few attempts, others were like that they can't take this anymore after 3-4 failures. This kind of demotivation comes because we have attached ourselves too strongly to the outcomes especially while dealing with the tough odds.

Apart from this, the problem further increases when people even fear to dream and are afraid to set newer goals because of this very notion. This stupid idea makes you play safe, hence pushing you to live an average life. No doubt, Gandhi back then said "Full effort is full success". But 99 % of people around us have never got this idea in a real sense. 190 years 1 month and 23 days of British rule and its ultra capitalistic operations in India, have mutated the DNA of Indian society. Hence people appreciate material possessions and tangible outcomes more than anything else. On other hand, your spiritual elevation; your wisdom as a result of struggle; your influence on others who will look up to you during their struggle phase and those who will now dare to take risks like you; your intangible acquisitions as a result of your daring efforts, all these hardly means anything for a lot of people in the Indian society and that is the most unfortunate thing. While Tibetan society holds such people in very high regard.

I believe that in the realm of ideas, wide acceptance and appreciation for "efforts" in an autonomous way, is an idea of the future. But not far future!

XIX

PART 2: A COLLECTION OF MY POEMS

MY MONOLOGUE

He held my hand,

And asked me to walk,

I fell, I crawled, I cried,

I resisted, I succumbed,

I hated him, I loved him,

Amidst his brutal anger,

There was strange warmth in him,

Beneath his deadly eyes,

Was a strange passion,

That lean man,

Carried a massive weight,

Of decades old, lost blood, of his father

And poured it on a young fragile me,

He went,

Reckless and insane,

I walked, when I couldn't

I crawled, when I couldn't

I stood awoke, when I couldn't,

He pulled me, he pushed me,

He taught me to walk,

And run and leap and fly,

Brutal he was,

Older I grew and I saw,

His childhood tears, he never shed,

Heard those words, he never spoke,

And,

With shortage of tools,

I learnt to climb,

In that shortage of space,

I created my place

Amidst the usual noise

I learnt to sit deaf,

I learnt to leap, and to sprint,

On my climbs, when I looked beneath

He would be there,

With his eyes of passion,

With his eyes of fury,

Small those hills,

I climbed again,

I won again,

That day on the way up,

When I saw beneath,

He was not there,

He was gone

And the climb became scary,

Yet I climbed,

Yet I won.

I was climbing for years now,

And the time had come,

For which we had started,

That massive hill,

That high invisible, misty peak,

It was the climb I hated,

It was the climb I loved,

And what to say,

That thunder, that storm,

In a pulse of clock,

I fell off the hill,

Brutally injured,

I saw to my left and I saw darkness,

To the right I saw, and it was a strange emptiness,

Behind I saw, and I was dead alone,

Front I saw, and I lied there,

Where I began 2 years ago,

I had fallen deep,

Deep down,

I started again, I climbed,

I reached on the top, what glory it was,

Standing above those clouds,

Those wind brought to me,

The vapors of his tears,

From miles away, and miles beneath,

And then,

I moved further,

It was a final climb now, a different hill,

Many feared that hill,

Many were consumed by it

It was a hill, way to brutal,

Brutal than him,

Amidst my solitude,

Amidst my fatigue,

That sun reflected his light,

That sky delivered me,

A piece of his soul,

And I crawled and I walked

I ran, I climbed,

For 9 years I climbed,

Insane, reckless,

My body numb,

And I for some,...dumb,

The efforts accumulate to more than a tone,

My blood, my sweat, my bones, my muscles,

They all turned into one,

I started this journey with many buddies,

While they left, with those frowns,

Following their knockdowns,

I stayed on the hill.

Earth revolved around the sun 6 times,

I stayed on the hill.

Moving , crawling , climbing,

The cliff, the peak was nearer,

I saw it sharp and clearer,

It was the final rugged phase,

Over that,..wild, wild chase,

The feet were all bruised,

They had pushed me,

More than they could,

There was hardly any flesh left,

Trust me, they were all wood,

But still my heart asked them,

"Let the boulders become carnivore

Keep going!

Just a little more

Just a little more"

So they pushed me up

And I took hold of a rock

I moved slowly,

Up that hill block,

Suddenly a boulder blade,

Pierced the wood of my feet,

Deep, very deep, indeed,

I saw no blood,

All I felt was a reckless pain,

Breathless, I halted, and my heart talked,

It said

"Remember the promise you made,

Back then, one and half decade,

You may halt and the wound may heal,

And a healed you, may climb again,

But let me tell you,

This halt,....you must refrain,

For the word you gave, for the word you kept,

Else, your soul shall ache, your soul shall pain,

That climb, that sweat, will all go in vain"

So I took his words,

And played the gamble,

The feet were dead,

And the hands, ochre red,

I did away with, the mental clog,

But hardly had I realized,

That the mist had turned into fog,

I moved and moved,

But then,

In just one motion stroke,

The boulder I held, suddenly broke,

This time the hill had no refuge,

Something worked like a subterfuge,

For one last time,

Through that fog,

I saw the peak, from a distance nearby,

The violent wind was singing a strange lullaby,

Down I went, freely I fell,

Like drowning in stream of air, it felt,

My bruised hand,

Curled around that sight of near-by peak,

All I had was air,

In that hand of teak,

Down I went,

I freely fell

And

As I went down the peak went farer and farer,

The falling me, tried to touch the sky,

And I told it,

Nothing is finished by,

As I went down, in that pain,

The fog turned into mist again,

While falling,

I saw the blood mark on that hill,

Of my feet,

On my way, up the hill,

Falling, I saw that sky through the mist,

Was proudly looking down,

At a falling, brave deontologist,

Down I went and strange that peace,

Amidst that pain, I felt no, disparagement,

For my journey was a transcendent,

And yes, some part of me, felt magnificent,

Now my soul talked

"You kept my dignity intact", it said

"You may fall, but I will not let you die",

While falling, I told the sky

That you don't know my creed,

That you don't know my breed,

I am not pulverized,

Back I will militarize,

And I just tell you in concise,

Back I will rise.

Back I will rise.

I sunk and sunk,

In that stream of air,

With half open eyes

And may be illusion it was,

I saw him,..in the sky,

Suddenly I heard a noise below,

I looked beneath,

Mist of the Hill was gone,

But through the mist of my eyes,

I saw something blurred,

The branch of that tree of the hill,

I extended, my blood drenched hand,

I caught it,

And it caught me...

With a pint of life,

I hanged on that branch,

Up I pulled myself,

But with a single stroke,

That branch too broke,

Down again I went in that stream of air,

But I had a piece of branch in my hand,

I broke it, into two,

And with all my life and roaring scream,

I threw one, opposite to the hill,

The 'third law' worked,

And I went down,

Dragging against the hill,

Numb as I was,

With that second branch piece,

I pierced the veins of that hill,

And it pierced that of mine

I dredged its soil,

And it drenched me, with my blood,

Suddenly I halted,

And while hanging on that hill,

I pulled myself up and collapsed.

A rock lied in front of me,

The same rock, on which I had inscribed,

On my way up, years ago.

While lying there I wiped its dust

It said

"No matter what the pace

All my life,

I have always finished my race"

And I stood up and moved,

And I climbed,

And climbed,

And climbed…

AGAIN A KNOCKDOWN

Again a knock down,

And a smile turned into a frown,

At 1:30 AM,

UPSC turned me red and brown,

And what to say,

Again..... I am in a "little" dismay,

A year was gambled yet again,

Again I missed the train,

But strangely,

There is no significant pain,

I am so accustomed, so accustomed,

To this furious rain,

It's a strange kind of impermeability,

But somehow I know the art of equanimity,

And

For my passion, for that hill top,

8 years,

Those 8 years of climb,

It was some damn raring,

It was a............. "Rare daring",

I had gambled so much,

Preposterously,

And yes Mr. Osho,

That is the real "joy of living dangerously"

And what to say........

I attempted my passion, with some drastic improvement,

With a mind, more than ever efficient,

And to my utter, utter astonishment,

Still,

Still there is no sign of rapprochement!

.......................Except, except this UPS(ee),

So many voices, are pulling me,

And my sweet mom says,

Let us continue the spree,

Let us fight till the end,

Let us give, another pre,

I do wonder

My journey and this blood on my feet,

Does this effort,...weighs more than,

Those sweats of that laborer, on my street

I wonder, I wonder

So many queries!!

So many questions!!

Oh dear heart,

Let's not find an answer today,

Temporarily though,

Let's stop all the experimentations,

Let there be a little procrastination,

Let us wait for the reconfiguration,

Oh dear heart,

Let me walk into the hills yet again,

Let us halt, at those "serais",

Let me think,

About that Japanese Ikigai.

Let the questions prevail

Let me walk over a joyful trail

For a while,

Let the questions prevail!

INTERSTELLAR

It's so bizarre,

That South Korean music queen,

And that Bollywood star,

I hear about suicides,

And my mind goes on a questioning ride,

Just wait and think,

How lucky we are?

At the peak of the sapien civilization,

We took birth,

Were we born in times of Khiljee,

Could we enjoy those 3 D movies,

And those burgers with extra chee(se),

A million candidates for that embryo, there were,

And we won the lucky draw,

That embryo turned into magnificent us,

Into a being,

With flesh and blood,

With eyes to see this beautiful world,

But one condition did god impose,

You have limited time on this planet,

So live,... your life to the fullest,

But Still!

Still, they do that,

I often wonder

I often ponder,

There is so much noise,

And turbulence in heads around,

Those other words become important,

And our own authentic self, sinks down,

Please

Get out of this noisy deluge,

Life is short and world is huge,

What we face, is the crisis of gratitude,

Cherish the trees, the birds and the moon,

And yes..

These problems and anguishes,

And their deadly ambushes,

Look a little behind,

They were creations of our own mind,

So,

Halt oh man!

Halt a little,

See the millions of stars around,

And somewhere, in this interstellar,

We are in a thin, beautiful lamellar,

Just think; just think... how lucky we are!

YO MECHANCHEE!

One for all, and all for one,

That fraternity, that camaraderie,

Those mass bunks, those roars,

To that ground hall of auditorium,

We inherited a "STRICT NO'

For it allowed, only silent humans,

So we rocked, on that upper balcony,

Which saw many, our generations come,

And many of ours go,

That workshop of ours,

That SAE, That race BAJA

Building our cars, and rolling on foreign lands,

Eating food, by the side of those boilers,

And with our gears, and our pistons,

We pumped the blood of university,

We talked in Horse Power,

We talked in C.C.,

And what to say,

That Crisis of girls,

And aching of distances,

Less was our romance,

And more was our "Bromance",

And let it be known, of our creed,

Come may,

The time to prove our blood,

You will see a thermal combustion,

Without a refrigerant,

Without a coolant,

More exo,

Less endo,

And let me tell you without a sigh,

When we screw,

Even the metals cry.

I SAW MYSELF

An awesome weather today, it was,

My bike wanted to taste the weather too,

How could I say no to it?

So I drove,

Aimless, I drove,

I went there where my bike took me,

Elephant like memory it had,

It took me to PEC, probably its favorite place,

We entered its gate,

And suddenly....... it reduced its pace,

I saw PEC again,

As usual, it was noisy and dynamic,

Even Wuhan, failed to silence it,

I heard the same cheers in its playground,

And I saw,

That 9 years, younger me,

Putting fresh feet on those stairs of my college,

With joy and ecstasy, as if it was some privilege,

I moved ahead and I drove,

I saw myself on that lane,

Chasing my buddy,

On that festival of Holi,

And oh!

That sacrosanct place,

But I was amazed,

That heart of PEC,

That booth was razed,
And,

That massive yellow library door,

My same old friend,

Said "Hi" to me,

And we moved further,

And we saw that mechanical block,

Where....Where I used to rock,

Nearby

I saw myself,

Addressing those juniors,

Near those admin stairs,

That.... that Rotary affair,

And just nearby,

I saw myself standing,

By that helicopter, and by that train,

Peeping through that tutorial class,

.... that broken window frame,

And in that market, at that Xerox shop,

For those exams, it was our single, solo hope,

Finally

With the lot of memories,

We left,

My bike was still not tired,

It took me to my secondary school,

I saw myself playing cricket and football,

Those walls on which I pasted my election posters,

And talking to my dearest Italian Principal,

There she said, "Neither doctor neither engineer"

And

I saw an adolescent me,

Who knew nothing, what to do in life,

Who knew not,

About any struggle or strife,

And then I left for my home,

But those pleasant winds cooled,

The radiator of my bike,

And it was still,

Still full of life,

So we went to my senior secondary school,

A place of my final showdown,

Since last two years,

And I saw a 10 year younger me,

Climbing those walls,

And running away at full speed,

Those memories, beautiful, beautiful indeed,

It was dark,

And my bike finally agreed,

So we ended our short journey

Sometimes it's ok to escape

From life's odyssey,

To reclaim and cherish,

Our old pristine journey.

ALI

That power of Tyson,

That style of Foreman,

But there existed a legendary man,

He went in to the ring, "pretty",

And he came out "pretty",

His senses, so rare and witty,

A risk taker, a rebel,

Like butterfly he floated,

And like bee he would sting,

More than a boxer,

Less than some God,

Inside the ring, he punched his rivals

Outside the ring,

He attacked the apartheid fluvials,

He stood by his conscience,

And stood behind the bars

And so politely, took numerous scars

Lost his title, lost his belt,

Again he returned,

And reclaimed his glory, amidst those stone pelts,

Alone he stood, Alone he walked,

Crazy this man,

For he risked his life,

In that ring, for his passion,

With Parkinson's, he fought, when every blow

A ticket, to the heavens mansion,

His rival Frazier, that "Thrilla",

In that deadly ring of Manila,

I saw a living God,

Fine they hail Tyson's uppercut,

Or Fraziers left hook,

Or Shaver's power punch,

But he, the master of none,

And yet a rare one,

The will to endure the hardest blow,

And fight with numb body,

While his energy drained, while his life flowed,

Their lied his greatness,

Their lied his godliness.

THE SILENT AUTUMN

A strange autumn it is,

There is a rain of leaves,

On these silent streets,

That cover of yellow glare,

First time,

They lie in peace,

On the otherwise noisy streets,

The autumn birds are bewildered,

As suddenly,

A lot has altered,

As they see the humans tethered,

A strange autumn it is!

A silent autumn it is!

CIVIL OBEDIENCE

It was a massive civil disobedience then,

And there is some civil disobedience now,

Then, it was by the patriots,

And now, either by the fools,

Or by some real destitute,

Long ago,

He asked them, to come out in the streets,

And break that "immoral law",

Now again I see those noisy streets,

As they break the "moral law",

In that civil disobedience,

His stick was in fact a glorious insignia,

And now,

Oh Lord!! These clowns,

They know well, about that deadly stick,

..Of those "Men in browns",

But still they disobey, still they disobey,

This much needed lockdown!

Long ago

The people in that civil disobedience,

Endured the brutal blows,

Glorious it was,

Even as their blood flowed,

And Now,

A little despondency,

And some real impatience,

Now, it's either a pressed,

Or a real silly, civil disobedience,

And yes with the same outcome

Those Laathi blows on the bum!

Long ago,

It was "Dandi" then,

And it's "Dand" with the "Dandas" now,

Long ago

He went to get salt on that seashore,

And,

The law stood broken,

Now they talk about, an old humble man,

Roaming on streets and asking for food and salt,

He showed disobedience, they say,

For the law stood broken!!

Long ago

On "That person's call"

They had locked down their daily living,

Voluntarily though,

They gave their hand to his civil disobedience,

And now,

There is again a lock down, of the daily living,

Not voluntarily though,

But for that, much needed call,

That call for "Civil Obedience",

Long ago,

He was fighting the "imperialism virus",

And now,

We are fighting some real deadly virus,

Long ago,

His civil disobedience was against a mighty nation,

A strange, this déjà vu,

Civil disobedience, by those few,

Has worsened the situation, of that same nation,

Of its Royalty, and now even Boris Johnson,

Long ago

On the planes of morality,

That civil disobedience was definitely good,

And now,

This one, by these few, is really dangerous,

And it is not well understood,

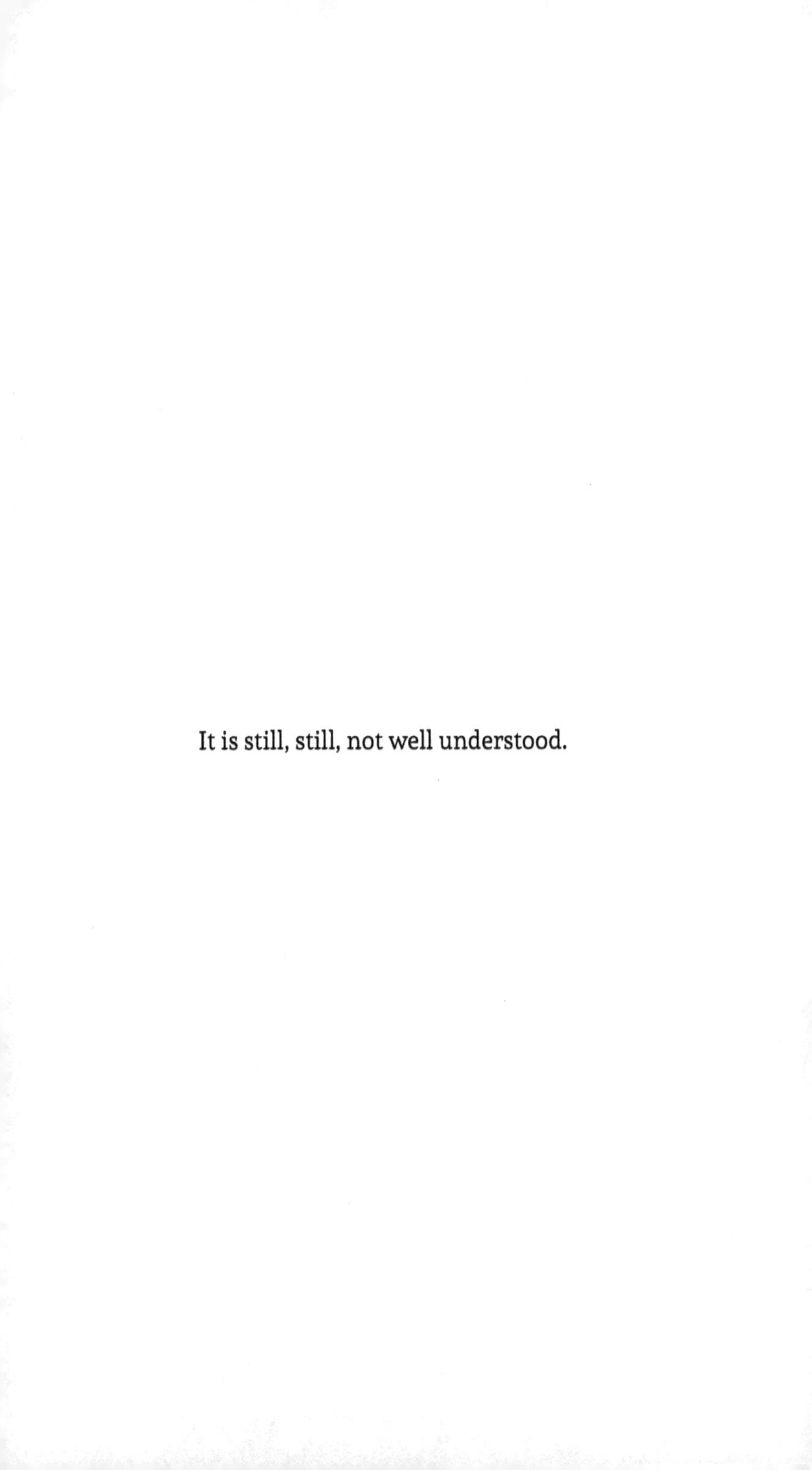

It is still, still, not well understood.

TERRACE OF MY HOUSE

Years after,

I sat on the terrace of my house,

For so long,

I had never stepped on it

Strange, this maze of life

Sometimes,

Something so dear,

Is so very near,

But yet becomes so far,

And it's so very bizarre,

Years after,

Years after I sat on the terrace,

In silence, I observed

The beautiful hills in the north,

That shrine in the east,

That vegetation in the west,

Those roof water tanks, in the south,

Those memories of my childhood beneath my feet,

That old clear sky above me,

And yes,

I found that junk

That old antenna in dust,

That mess, my dad used to adjust,

In search of that signal

And that noise "ticktack",

Long after I saw that antenna, and I got a flashback,

A child me, shouting to dad,

That "Yes dad, yes, "Aa gaya signal",

That old voice of mine, I felt so very glad,

Hhh...

That terrace,

Those memories,

My old friend, that plant sapling,

Which once, with all its daring,

Made its way through the wall cracks

Was no longer there,

Probably it lost to the new concrete pack,

And,

That pure cold wind,

In whose search,

I travelled to the hills time and again,

And it's strange to explain,

I forgot, I forgot,

That the same pure air,

Blew on the terrace upstairs,

The terrace of my house,

It was so near me,

Yet remained far away from me,

All these years,

I had climbed so much,

But, that small ladder,

Got skipped from my mind,

A small, small distance,

Strangely,

I forgot to climb!!!

LUCY

I move out of my house,

And I fear her bite,

I look from the balcony,

And I love that sight,

Of hers feeding those,

Two brown pieces of my heart,

Their cute noises,

Their love for their mother,

And in my neighborhood,

That cute little girl,

That Mom of Lucy, and grand mom of her puppies,

So sweet that little girl,

She feeds them, she caresses them,

But that insane barking and biting,

And that animal won't stop,

Under the sun,

She hunts every passerby,

Under the moon,

She barks recklessly and feeds on my sleep,

And the day I feared came,

My Dad, the hater of dogs,

My Dad, the Indian "Chandler",

My Dad: the strict policeman,

Was almost bitten by Lucy,

And he gave a call,

And those fed up souls, stood by him,

But that little girl, that mom, that grand-mom,

Was left alone,

My heart was with her,

But that silly mind, went with dad,

And then I saw the dog catcher truck,

And what to say,

Like all my life, the heart won,

And I prayed,

Oh blood thirsty Bitch!

Please don't show up.

They searched the street,

Below the cars, in the corners,

Strangely that day,

Even, dust of her feet was invisible,

They waited and waited

And went back,

I had a sigh of relief,

And I stood there gauging,

And oh wow! I shouted,

Great that connivance,

I saw, what that little girl did there!,

She protected her deadly kid,

And her cute grandkids,

Up, she saw at me,

And lowered her eyes,

She forgot, I had my Dad's flesh,

Not his soul,

But Lucy's fury remained the same,

And Dad picked up the phone again,

In the first light of my morning,

I heard the cries of Lucy,

Down I ran,

Helpless that little girl looked at me,

Her kid lied in the net,

And all they, had a sigh of relief,

With a heavy heart,

I asked him to set herfree,

My mother pulled me back,

Yet I blocked the truck,

What pain it was,

In front of all, I fought my mother,

That fury was released,

And truck went back,

I looked down from there.

And I saw those brown pieces of my heart,

Feeding on Lucy,

And an hour later,

Lucy chasing a passerby,

Difficult sometimes it is,

To decide on,

The clash of two rights,

For you are always are wrong,

But still yet right!

THE HOOKER

Up the shoulders of Kufri,

I climbed,

That muddy steep hill,

With neither a dyke nor a sill,

And those apple trees,

With those small red pearls,

Slept beneath that white blanket,

For they feared the wrath of sky,

And through them, I climbed,

To reach that hill top,

Shaped like a rock table,

And those endless horses,

Just like an open stable,

A ride they gave,

To the easy goers,

To that Mahasu peak,

But that joy on my feet,

I had always seek(ed),

But his time I had company,

Those horses.... and we started together,

A horse man,

Offered me a ride,

And his prices went down

Slide and slide,

The path was a muddy deluge,

And I couldn't refuse,

But hardly I knew,

An exam was adieu,

A test of integrity,

While riding the horse,

He offered,

A prostitute on the hill top,

And a war began in my heart,

Between,

The wild bear and the wise lion,

While that horse climbed,

The white lion was invincible and the black bear strong,

The blood flew, in that battle,

within my heart,

And the lion won,

For I had nourished him,

Entire my life,

I refused to weigh her body with those paper green,

Atop the hill I reached,

So crowded,

As if a secluded city,

Away from that military barrier,

And of course that shrine,

Amidst that noise unexpected,

I felt proud with my spoken NO,

With a strange feel of goodness,

I stood on the ridge of that hill,

I stood upright on the ridge of the hill.

DECADE COMES TO AN END

The decade comes to an end,

At the sounding hour of the decade,

It was all about those institutions,

The IIT, the BITS, the PEC,

Their goal and my illusion,

That illusion......that delusion,

For me, it was an idiotic spree,

And what to say!..I got all the three,

They were a dream for some, but still I wasn't free,

Then my heart discovered itself,

It wasn't there, but somewhere else,

So I left and walked,

On a road of mine, and that distant destiny,

The road was mine, I was all happy,

In the face of circumstances,

I played my symphony,

And ya!..many called it a bit crazy,

It was a road less travelled,

And I avoided all the cacophony,

And yes!, I discovered the real me,

That zeal for the East, and that skill of pedagogy,

Yes Mr. Rudyard, I understood the game,

Definitely sir, triumph and disasters are mere imposters,

They have to be treated, just the same,

Wow This decade!

I had climbed the walls; I had climbed the hills,

Through those chills, through that mist,

Of dear decade you gave me a rare gift,

An opportunity to struggle and opportunity to discover,

To find that,

What they are late to uncover,

Oh dear decade, I owe you so much,

I will remember your autumns; I will remember your springs,

Thanks for everything, Thanks for everything.

THE OLD MAN IN THE PARK

That lush green park,

With a fountain beneath,

With its towering lights,

Like a day in the night,

The symphony of singing birds,

The moves of that dancing group,

That joy of juveniles,

Those broken swings,

That talking and laughing a loud,

Of the white haired men,

Their congregation,

As if a daily ritual,

I go to the park,

For a daily delight,

But amidst the vigor of life,

I saw an on old man

Alone he would sit,

On the same bench,

Nor to the left, not to the right,

Day and every day,

Back and forth his head would move,

Doing nothing,

Talking nothing,

Just sitting,

Just observing

A Senile insane,.. Was he?

Weeks and months passed,

We didn't talk,

And I would just walk,

But my curiosity was up till the brim,

The man talked,

And, gold he uttered,

A strange sense of depth he had,

My end is near, Said he,

He was doing, he never did,

Spending time with self,

To enjoy the vibes of silence,

Amidst the very mild noise,

To find answers, to some questions,

I hear and heard,

But one day he vanished,

Days passed, months passed,

The Bench lied empty and I sat on his spot,

recalled his words, And his voice,

That tone of his regret,

And a hoards of frets,

I realized,

He wasn't alone with that grief,

Me and the passerby's,

With that stupid ignorance deep beneath,

Were treading his path, a brief,

As Life takes you on a busy ride,

And you forget its true purpose,

I see a crisis,

A deep wild crisis,

Of a little halt,

Of silence in solitude

Of gratitude,

Of love with the infinity,

Of serendipity,

Hence I went to home,

And now I sit in silence,

And see the world,

Through my window frame

And now it's their turn,

To call me, a stupid insane.

GRANDMOTHER

Frail and short,

In that room she sits,

Her favorite place,

She forgets my name,

Not the name of god,

She forgets my mother,

Not the name of god,

She forgets the way to eat,

Not the name of god,

She stands near her bed

With the name of god, she bows her head,

It's not the Gurudwara, I say,

Strange looks she gives me back,

Hence again I defray,

Strange that disease,

It feeds on her memories,

Living in the city house,

She thinks it as her village house,

Amidst my pity for her,

I revile in her non-sense talks,

From my city neighborhood,

She asks me to call her village neighbors,

She lives her past,

In this present,

And gives me a 4 decade old task,

I know not, what to say,

She asks to call over the people,

Who now lay dead,

And Sometimes,

She thinks, mother as her childhood friend,

Then I see her along with my dad,

Once she had taught my dad to eat,

Now I see him, teaching,

The right way to eat,

It's the phenomenon, so rife

It's the..

It's the circle of life.

KHEERGANGA

Amidst the noisy chiseling,

Of those green hills,

Beneath that sunny weather,

That wind, blew,

Deprived of its chills,

Steep down, I walked,

For,

A descent always precedes,

A glorious climb,

...And I began a long journey,

Up that hill,

Me with me,

Into the mysteries of those renowned hills,

They knew my creed,

Spoke they,

"Again you come

And quite strange your daring,

You don't fear my ghoul,

Again you bring, just,

..Just your soul",

I laughed and walked,

Through those friendly deodars,

Next to that friendly death,

And oh yeah!

I got some company,

Of those three,

The broken heart,

The cheer some,

And the relentless,

Each carrying some piece of me,

Amidst,... my solitude,

I relished, their aura,

Delightfully I walked,

Besides them,

On that dusty trail,

And strange that hill,

Like a lazy chameleon,

It changed its color,

Slowly, very slowly,

The brown of that dust,

Turned white,

The dread of that gorge ,

Was now loud,

Death was now blue,

That fearsome roaring brook,

Flowing just beneath my feet,

"So again we meet"

I said,

"Many more times to come"

It said,

Opposite may be, but,

We moved next to each other,

And strange that hill,

Its trail became frail,

Thinner, and ever thinner,

And what a dark magic,

White of the ice turned black,

As if threatening me,

And what to say,

In a pulse of moment,

All I heard was a sound 'shoo',

And I got same real déjà vu,

Down I collapsed,

And the "Black" of that white,

Had nearly,

Consumed me,

But that giant friend of mine,

Like always,

Gave a refuge to me,

And I moved further,

Piercing the silence,

Over that steep-steep hill,

Through those dark green woods,

And we walked and walked,

And reached a place,

Where sky was deficient,

And the mountains, abundant,

The moon, deficient,

And the stars, abundant,

The green, deficient,

And the white, abundant,

The air, deficient,

But its purity,..abundant,

My breath, deficient,

But at same time,...abundant,

It was a land of scarcity,

Yet a land of abundance,

Where,

I stood all the way up,

Above that sun,

But below,

That white downpour,

It was a land of miracle,

Where flowing hot water

Melted the sheet of snow,

I had climbed.

Into the soothing arms,

Of those hills,

And amidst those thrills,

And the,

Damn wrecking chills.

There was a strange warmth,

A renowned warmth.

BUGYAL OF KHAJJIAR

Amidst those mountains of Chamba,

Lies this beautiful green Bugyal,

When I walk under the sun,

I feel heat a little more,

When I walk into the shades of fir,

I feel chills a little more,

In that sky,

I see those flying men,

Those gliders, piercing the clouds,

Below I see,

The sparkling dew on that grass,

I walked and walked,

And reached a shrine,

And yet again, a new déjà vu,

Of the previous trails,

Of those earlier treks,

Be it Dainkund,

Or the Triund,

A little perplexed I am,

A religion always adorns,

The top of every peak,

And,

Amidst those noisy boys

In those rolling toys,

Amidst those herb sellers,

I stood with my eyes closed,

And heard the tunes,

Of those chirrs,

Of those birches,

And of those firs,

I stood,

With my eyes closed.

DAINKUND

To the crass voice of 4:00 AM clock,

I walked towards the hills alone,

No accompany, no flock,

I reached there

That market in the hills,

Traded in wood,

But a route passed by,

Adorned by tall silent woods,

To that place called Dainkund,

That road, I traversed,

Up the hill, me with me,

The woods seemed amazed,

And closely they gazed,

"Don't you fear my bears" they said?

"Don't they fear the wild-wild me", I said,

They laughed,

And the amiability grew,

Those engines, carrying the easy doers,

Passed by a few,

Their smoke as if curse,

To me and the woods,

But amidst that natures lapse,

I walked and walked,

And I saw the peak of Dainkund,

A trail of concrete,

Ran up like a red carpet,

To their cabin of glory,

From the cabin, I saw five mountains,

Covered in green,

And Clouds beneath,

But their heads above the sky,

That man offered that liquid brown drug,

I refused, he freaked

For I have always hated the tea,

That gentle wind,

Took every drop of my sweat,

And I lied on the grass,

Full with life, yet like a dead,

Doing nothing,

Thinking nothing,

In the arms of that hill,

I slept and slept.

JIBHI

Down in the lapses of valley Tirthan,

Lies a small town,

A step forward I take,

The town ends,

A step back I take,

The town starts,

Loitering around,

I heard a sound,

And chased it,

In a subtle astound,

Through the mist,

I walked

To that pond,

And it's clear, white water,

The natures subtle chatter,

Stepping the stones,

Into that stream,

I reached a place of god,

That waterfall,

And that rainbow emerging,

From that water green,

Such a place,

My ears had never heard,

My eyes had never seen.

RAGHUPUR FORT TREK

Up those highs,

Up that lake Sirloskar,

And beneath that Jalori sky,

Into the woods, I walked,

Through those walnuts, through those pines,

On a trail,

To that ruins of fort medieval,

Up that steep hill,

Lied a green tiny grassland,

I stopped by,

Too humane, too invaded,

Some playing music,

Some dancing in a group,

And some smoking weed,

Nice warm scenes, nice warm scenes,

But I didn't came across,

What I always looked for,

For my spellbound,

My astound,

Was still a little away,

And with my buddy around,

I took the trail,

And far into the woods,

We walked,

And reached a grassland,

With grazing cows,

And a beautiful lake,

I saw those people,

Shy of modernity,

And with a gaze of curiosity,

They looked at us,

And with a friendly gaze we looked,

We talked and oh what the hell!

I was lost in the woods,

For we took a wrong trail,

But I sat there

Near those grazing cows,

Those old sweet ladies and,

That delicacy of their snacks,

I walked all over and started a fresh,

It was getting dark,

Still I climbed,

Breathless I climbed,

To reach those beautiful ruins,

Up that sky,

I saw a young emerging moon,

And of course that shrine,

With those bells and their chimes,

I walked on the fort walls,

Through that fog through that mist,

My feet were bruised,

But my soul was renewed,

In that cloud I sat

And thanked the hills,

For I got lost,

Though my feet, took the cost,

And then the hill spoke

My ignorance, it really broke,

Said she

"If you don't lose track,

If you don't waste time,

How'll you find,

Your real joys.......and your real rhymes."

GILBERT TRAIL

That romance with the hills,

The glance of that trail,

Except,

Those insects murmuring,

And those birds chirping,

And the crass thumps,

Of my feet walking,

I heard not anything,

With my friend, that soaring hill,

On one side,

And valley of death on other,

I walked through the clouds,

On a thin-thin trail,

Beneath that summer in the sky,

And through chills of the clouds,

I walked and walked,

With my eyes turning moist,

Were they overwhelmed?

For they saw,

What they, never had dreamt,

Or was it the chill of those clouds?

As they floated pass me,

The answer I knew not

But then I came across,

A fallen tree,

Blocking the trail,

As if nature saying,

There is danger ahead,

So I jumped

And walked further,

But then, the trail vanished,

And that deep death,

Merged with my friend,

I stopped and looked at my friend,

Said I,

"Will you hold me", if I fall?

"Of course my lion", it said,

And,

On its body, I crawled slant,

Hhh...That dread,

And her constant tingling on my waist,

It said, If you fall,

You shall vanish into infinity,

Into my green serendipity,

I listened and listened

I laughed and crawled,

And maybe she felt trolled,

For I found the trail again,

I walked through the mist again,

Alone I walked,

Through the heaven of my friend,

Singing to my symphonies,

And talking to those birds,

I walked and walked,

On that trail,

...The Gilbert trail.

THE WOODS OF MASHOBRA

I reached that town,

But I felt like a clown,

For that place,

Was still at a distance,

With some vague directions,

I walked,

Into the woods yet again,

The trail took me down,

And what to say,

He looked into my eyes,

And, I looked at his furious fur,

For he sensed my fear,

It was right there in my eyes,

So very clear,

He waged his tail,

And we had a peace,

His polite bark,

As if asking me to follow him,

And the next second,

I was following him,

Through those woods,

On that path,

Something more than a trail,

And less than a road,

We walked and walked,

And with every step of descent,

A part of me,

Feared my way up,

And a part of me rejoiced,

The evening woods,

But we walked and walked,

And the roadside board,

Lifted my soul,

Those firs,

Neither too dense,

Nor too dispersed,

And then,

Amidst those juvenile murmurs,

My friend,

My guide, returned back,

I wish I could touch his fur,

And bid a warm adieu,

Then I walked a little more,

And I reached,

That beauty at its full score,

That hut,

On verge of that green hill,

That furious dark cloud,

That distant orange sky,

And of course that shrine,

Those were the hills of Mashobra

The hospitality of the divine.

EDUCATION

It's about,

How to live and how to make a living,

And also about wholesome character building,

And drawing the best, out of spirit, mind and the body,

Like Shantiniketan and the Nai Talim of Gandhi,

It's not preparation for life, rather its life's basic premise,

It's not what to think rather how to think and analyze,

It requires better approach, and innovative policies,

Like Tuglaq Feroz, Sikandar Lodi........and their very legacies,

Said Malala,

One child, one teacher, one book, can change the world,

Like it pushed, Lincoln and Kalam to the zeninths fold.

HEALTH

Mind and body; heart and soul,

For a better power and for a better role,

Away from illness, and beyond mere wellness,

To attain real potentials and to live life to its fullness,

Healthcare ....it's about social justice and human right,

In "The ICMR report", why such dismal plight?

Better Initiative and less policy cholesterol,

Like legacies of..Tughlaq Feroz and Fidel Castro.

FARMER

Clad in shabby dress, drenched with sweat,

He drives the economies, He thrives the polities,

He fills the tummies, he feeds the factories,

On his dint lie numerous destinies,

But his destiny still lies on those winds: "south-westerlies"

From Asoka to Feroz , from Feroz to Akbar

The sector, was a core focus,

Ideation, innovation and acceleration,

Can really push up, it's growth curve locus.

INTEGRITY

Far away from materialism and far away from hedonism,

Neither cronyism, nor nepotism,

Thought, speech and action, all in synchronism,

Like the legend of Socrates and that cup of poison,

Dear public servant,.....It's all about integrity,

........That's your supreme religion.

DEMOCRACY

It is much beyond the Lincolns statement,

Its empowering populace with choice and liberty,

With quick on demand services delivery,

With due accountability and full responsibility,

With cannons of efficiency, economy and equity,

And yes upholding the idea of popular sovereignty.

NATURE

Be it the Harappan or Mayan civilization,

Nature worship is a long tradition,

Now, arms of clock have rendered fear,

Blue-white skies; no longer clear,

The threat is really not remote,

Worries that grieving fifth report (IPCC),

Sea waters once, awesome white,

Now cluttered with debris, that dismal sight,

Floods in deserts

And deserts in greens,

And Greens in white,

And whites in blue,

And look over there,

The planet is "in blues",

Our responsibility and Please!

No excuse!

Let's not make, the future generations accuse,

We need to Reduce, Recycle and Reuse,

Let's be sustainable,

Let's not overuse!

TOLERANCE

Numerous perspectives and numerous ideologies,

Respect the differences and cherish the similarities,

Let the coexistence be peaceful,

Like Ashoka's Dhamma and Akbar's Sulh-i-kul,

With tolerance, the world is really beautiful.

JUSTICE

Beyond tribunals and beyond Court of law,

It's about liberties, rights and opportunities,

And yes!.. Rule of law,

As the legends of Ashoka and Balban, speak,

It's about,

Empowering the humble and the weak.

XX

PART 3: THOUGHT OF THE DAY: A COLLECTION

- I don't trust anybody more than HRTC drivers (Himachal bus drivers). On my way to Barshaini from Kasol, the bus was traveling on a cliff hanger road (and it was damn narrow). Suddenly I noticed that a part of the tire of the bus was almost off the road and below lay a thousand feet deep valley. And when I cautioned the bus conductor, he said "we drive at 80 kmph in areas where there are no roads. So don't worry!"

- Ali was a greater boxer than Tyson. Even Tyson had accepted that.

- I think the most powerful realization of mine is "Life is short and the world is huge". Remember that!

- I do not completely agree with Osho, but the man made bloody sense.

- In that interview, they asked him, "When did Babur defeat Ibrahim Lodi?"He knew the answer. Then they asked, "How many unsuccessful attempts did he make to capture India. He didn't know the answer." Lesson: History remembers just one glorious victory and not the failed attempts.

- Patience is not an autonomous value. A person (especially for an aspirant) who can resist, sacrifice, persevere; who can walk alone; who has faith in the hope no matter how small it is, who can tolerate and ignore; who has command over his emotions and not vice versa; who is humble enough to accept his mistakes and ignorance; who can push himself when every cell of the body is fatigued, only such a person can show some real patience.

- Some people will understand only what they want to understand or just that, which places them in a good position. They will filter out the facts to suit their pre-established opinions. They make fool of their own conscience and makes it believe that righteousness lies on their side. Therefore the habit persists. And sometimes it is best to pity these petty creatures. Just move on and always remember: "Time always speaks".

- Always follow these great men and their qualities. Darings like Che Guevara; Integrity like Socrates; endurance like Mohammad Ali; idealism like Gandhi; Bravery like Lachit Borphukan and Guru Gobind Singh;

Realism and tolerance like Akbar; Courage of conviction like Jack ma.

- Sometimes it is a little difficult to wake up from bed and continue your journey and struggle. But once you overcome the bed, your whole day goes well.

- Society invests in our education, food, shelter, and all our basic needs. In return, it sometimes demands one thing from you. Your wisdom and common sense! Never agree to it. It's a very costly deal.

- I was told to respect and listen to our elders because that's an important part of Indian culture. I wanted to do a graduation in arts, but one day my parents called a person from the neighborhood (much elder to me and I call him "bhaiya"), he suggested to me and my parents that I should opt for engineering. The next day I was doing engineering. Now the engineering degree lies in my drawer and I am doi ng my beloved arts course. So while respecting your elders, always keep your brain with yourself.

- Wisdom is not the monopoly of age. Stupid uncles and elders are roaming around me.

- I think the best definition of religion is recognizing your duties as a divine command. And very importantly, while chalking out your duties, just use your reason, common sense, and your moral faculties.

- No one can defeat a man, who knows how to walk alone.

- Silence, these days, is taken as proof of culpability. Time will change. Soon.But not very soon.

- We create problems in our minds because we place ourselves at the center of the universe. But we forget that we are just quarks in this infinite universe.

- Don't worry if you are struggling! If you are a man of reason and morals, your silence is already creating massive respect for you, at least amongst the wise. The remaining are the fools, about whom you should hardly care about. So move on and continue!

- If you want to differentiate between a real and a fake philosopher, always remember that the real one will say great things in simple words and will live those words. The fake ones say great things in the complex language (because they are pirated) and will pretend to realize those words. Kindly learn the difference.

- Chona was more experienced than Christopher Columbus and had better technology and better caliber, but his King was not supportive of him. Columbus got the required support and he then discovered America. Therefore, no matter what caliber you have, your success is sometimes determined by the environment around you. So be careful about your environment!

- Even if in a room, keep your study/working table near a window. So that you can steal a few seconds of silence, from your work. Just look upon the trees, the sky, and the birds on the other side of window, keep a bowl of grains to feed the birds. They will visit quite often.

Watch them. It will remind you that you are mortal; it is the basis of gratitude and happiness.

- I often failed to do meditation regularly. But whenever I did, I understood that it routes the knowledge and intellect from the mind to every cell of the body. It ensures the realization of knowledge.

- Patience in mind and vigor in action can make you invincible.

- I never really felt ashamed of my knockdowns. Shame always comes in those people who are arrogant and narcissistic. These are the ones who commit suicides out of guilt and shame. Staying humble in your "up phase" of life vaccinates you against the germs of shame during your down phase. But don't think of a counter-example like Mohammad Ali. Boxing requires playing mind games.

- We often read great sayings but we do not realize them deeply. It takes some real struggle and meaningful silence to realize them. I once read the poem "IF" by Rudyard Kipling in a school poetry recitation contest. I understood very little of it. 15 years later I have realized that every word of it is pure gold, and it is probably the best poem ever written.

- Talk to random people; with passing rikshaw walas, burger sellers, cobblers, food delivery persons, street vendors, etc. Just be acutely humble and respectful of them. It is a free and great source of wisdom. It not only helps in understanding different perspectives of life but also makes them feel quite good.

- The day you will start appreciating the acting skills of Manoj Bajpayee and Nawazuddin over the so-called superstars of Bollywood; The day you will realize the greatness of Mikhail Tal; of Rahul Dravid; of Waseem Barelvi , give me a call, I will give you a free copy of this book of mine.

- Ambition, commitment, and determination are the guiding force for the right attitude.

- When you get overwhelmed with anger and frustration, go for a walk or write a poem.

- The sitcom "FRIENDS" should win a Noble peace prize for increasing the Gross global Happiness levels.

- Keep Laughing, keep moving, and keep improving.

- During your struggle for passion, many people may try to convince us that it is acute madness for what we are doing. Be careful! "Maximum people" saying such things are either envious or our ill-wishers and quite a few are talking just out of genuine concerns. Ignore! Strictly ignore! It is your passion and it is your dream. You have taken responsibility. You have to be aware that they are petty average humans. They don't know how humans evolve; they do not know that a bounce-back is always possible and the next level is possible. I used to call them "gobhi ke phool." You can have your names. If you allow their words to get into your head, the game will be over! So beware.

- Many a time there is another side of the story. And usually, it is the true one.

- They say "you are an average of 5 people with whom you spend most of your time". So be careful in choosing!

- One of my favorite quotes of Osho is, "Psychologists are the most stupid people on this planet. They think they can understand the mind."

- History is the most misunderstood subject in the world. Some call it dead, some call it useless. All Rubbish! History is a source of knowledge and wisdom. In your daily life, if you want an answer to any question, just delve deep into history and trust me, you will find an answer.

- Waste your time. It is important too..

- It is extremely important to put yourself in challenging situations. Under adversities and challenges, the true potential is unfolded. And if you do not know your true potential, life is a waste!

- Don't try to please people. You cannot succeed.

- Fear!! It is a natural thing. I have tried to defeat it at every moment of my life. But the day I was lost in the mountain jungles, near Jalori Pass, and that too under the descending sun, I fear nothing anymore!

- I need friends who let me be as crazy as I am.

- Bliss is..." in the hills, at a riverside camp, lying down on the cool grassy ground and reading Dr. Waseem Barelvi."

- Jaun Elia is a legendary poet, but a dangerous person to both watch and listen to. So be careful!

- It is so easy to know about people and make new friends. I once ordered food from a food delivery company at 4:00 PM (the empty hours of delivery people) and we talked for 5 minutes. He spoke about of few interesting things about his village but the best was about a ghost which beats utensils at the midnight, in front of the houses of people. What a Rajasthani conjuring!

- I like 3D goggles. While sitting on my chair, I can roam around the jungles of Africa and Latin America. If that is not the best invention by humans then what else is?

- I love the works of Rumi, Waseem Barelvi, and Ahmad Faraz. Interesting poets!!

- All my poor performances were mainly in the simplest of exams. And my best performances came when after the exam, other students cried. Now let me tell you something! I never really understood this dilemma.

- There are two kinds of people in academics. One who is street smart, and prepares the necessary portions for the upcoming exam. They are the ones who forget the concepts soon after the exam. And Second, are slow learners, but they retain, their knowledge for a whole lifetime. In 2019, a boy from the neighborhood came to me with a physics question from the eminent book of

H.C. Verma (Padma Shri). I had solved those questions 10 years ago. But still, I was able to solve one of the toughest questions of that chapter. I think I belong to the second category.

- A lot of people prepare for UPSC civil service exam, those who clear the exam, never accept that there is a luck factor involved. On other hand, the ignorant failures believe as if everything is about luck. But the truth is that the intersection of luck factor across the 3 phases of the exam amounts to a net luck factor of nearly 30-40 percent.

- Balban of Delhi Sultanate; Edward II of England; Rippon (British Viceroy in India); Muhammad Ali Pasha of Egypt and Subhash Chandra Bose....They are one of the most under-rated personalities in history.

- Sometimes love for a "dreadful" street dog and her puppies, can disrupt the half a century-old fraternity of a residential area. Moreover, fissures can be seen within families too. That is the power of love!

- Battle of Saraighat 1674 in Assam region; Battle of Chamkaur Sahib (1705) in Punjab region; Battle of Kondhana 1670 (Maharashtra); Cuban revolution 1958 and Vietnam war (1945 -1975), all have proven that whenever passions collide with superpowers, the passions have always won...Be passionate!

- Sometimes one may feel fine, but hurts do cause invisible and intrinsic damage within us. I realized this when I had a winning spree of 15 games in chess consecutively before the UPSC mains result and after the result, I lost 10 games consecutively.

- Today I was playing online chess with a person from some other nation. He played a good move, and texted me "It's over. India is an idiot". In the next few moves, I turned the game, and seeing a near checkmate he left the game and ran away. The lesson is that India is great and second don't conclude too soon!

- A startup should learn from Netflix. Just a few thousand employees and a multibillion dollar turnover! That's some real innovation.

- Go to the terrace of your house and gaze at the stars. It's the first step towards gratitude. And with gratitude, you can never feel low.

- They told us to accept the deaths of Homi Bhabha, Lal Bahadur Shastri, Benazir Bhutto . Martin Luther King Jr. as they were presented. Dear friends! I have a functional brain.

- Chandigarh!... More than its beauty, I like its organization.

- I like dropouts, for they finally break the fetters of societal demands and, they have finally learned to apply their brains.

- Western societies may have numerous vices, but if you work hard there, you get rewarded. Now please read this line two times more!

- I am a fan of Angelina Jolie....But after I saw the film "unbroken", directed by her, I am an even bigger fan now!

- We are those lucky people who are born at the peak of human civilization. So enjoy! We have a limited time.

- Whenever an argument happens, I realize that my mother is my dad's wife first and my mom later! And I don't like that.

- I have never tried to be better than anybody. I just tried to be at my best!

- Many people tell me that they didn't give up, just because of me. So that means there are even more people out there, who took inspiration from me because not everyone is grateful!

- I have my 29th birthday in 8 days and today my Mom asked me as to what I wanted as my birthday gift. I kept thinking for a while and I couldn't think of anything. Oh yeaah! how satisfied I am!!

- My real friends don't need explanations. So I keep moving, and they understand. That is real friendship.

- It's a struggle of my choosing and I often maintain my silence because I am at that level of struggle, where I have to find the answers myself. While a lot of them out there are amateurs.

- Those wise people call me humble; my friends call me crazy; those rebels call me their ideal; fools call me arrogant and idiots call me an idiot.

- I have kept walking through such milestones, which those people considered as their great achievements. (Inspired by a ghazal of Dr. Waseem Barelvi).

- After a setback, start afresh with what is easy and doable.

- Have patience! And the world will know.

- Try to be good on social media. And it's a two-minute job. Hence I see the world going crazy to present their digital best. Try to be good in real life. And it's a lifetime job. It feels good, but I find myself alone here.

- 190 years of British rule has created a notion that anything spoken in English is correct and superior. Try to analyze a scuffle between individuals in India, the moment one starts yelling in English, the other feels subjugated.

- Reiki... it's a damn interesting concept! A hoax to some, a reality to some, magic for some. But the fact is that the only feeling, that somebody is trying to heal you, actually heals you.

- Bolivia had already taken up socialist reforms but still Che Guevara continued with his battle. Sometimes you just continue, because you have nowhere to go.

- I am struggling like hell, right now, and I just realized that today is 14

- May 2021. Exactly 10 years before, I had achieved my trio goal of getting into IIT, BITS, and PEC. It was a daring struggle. At this point, I was walking out of the BITS examination hall in Mohali, with a tight lifted fist. Hhhh. It has been 10 years... I must continue!!

- The subject of Chemistry had got me through IIT and BITS. And in AIEEE 2011, I had probably secured one of the highest marks in India. And now I think that chemistry optional could have gotten me through UPSC civil services exam much earlier. I regret, not taking it as an optional. I regret!!

- Someone asked me my religion and I replied, "For 13 years I had read the verses of the Bible every day in the morning; I have grown up amongst Hindu friends; I have lived in a house made by Muslims and I am born into a Sikh family. So ask me a different question buddy!"

- I don't need education from stupid people. They teach me things, with which they have made a mess of their own lives. And the interesting fact is they don't even know.

- I have a habit of teaching students for a month or so after UPSC mains. This time also, I had taught those students for a month. And under compulsions when I couldn't continue anymore, I invited a friend teacher to replace me. Today he left the job and it's not even 1 month. He called me up and said, "Those students have made my life miserable and they don't let me teach. They are damn possessive about you". I sympathized with him. But, oh yes!! My soul is jumping with joy!

- I like a free press and objective reporting. Therefore I often go to YouTube for some authentic news reporting.

- "Cheats", give a rhythm to your quest. Friday outings for movies and Wednesday outings for junk food were two of my major cheats. COVID has blocked both of them. I hate COVID! I hate Wuhan!

- Eminent corporate usually offer their products for free (for quite some while). Then they start charging us. Gradually, the charges go up and up. Now if you know, people are lured into drugs in a similar manner. Isn't it?

- People are not afraid to play. They are afraid of losing.

- I see a lot of people following the path of spirituality when they are old. It's of no use. Spirituality has to begin early, in your life. Spirituality is not an extreme concept like penance or asceticism. Every moment of your life should be blended with the right proportion of spirituality.

- Today somebody told me a fantastic thing. He said, "Continue with what you are doing, just remove your brain from your mind". Oh, that's some damn real advice I've gotten in years!

- If you are constantly aware that you have a limited amount of time and energy on this planet, you will not waste even a second for stupid thoughts and stupid people. Your time is way too precious.

- Amidst the COVID crisis, they said, "nature is retaliating." It didn't go down well with me. Now after this cyclone Tauktae, I see that ocean has returned all the garbage to the shores....Now, I am in some real deep thinking.

- Today I was taking an afternoon nap. Mother came rushing into my room and broke the news of the death of a distant relative. And she started crying. He was quite dear to both of my parents. Of course, I got a little sad but I remained in the same sleeping posture and I asked my mother to remain calm. Since I didn't react the way she wanted me to react, she shouted at me and angrily asked me to keep sleeping. She closed the door strongly and walked away. How do I tell her that I am practicing the concept of equanimity!

- Never irk, never regret, never apologize for going beyond the levels of the comfort zones of other people.

- It is sad to see my friends struggling in those private companies. Many companies have an ethical work culture but some want to kill your awareness and consciousness by demanding better work productivity, more no. of working hours (and that too illegally). Beware, it's a bad deal!

- People who live after their deaths were not rich, they were men of consciousness.

- I have been a dropout many times in my life. Now I am a dropout from conventionalism and mob behavior.

- It's heart-wrenching to see these private hospitals exploiting the helpless COVID patients. The strongest man on this planet can feel helpless when his/her relative is dying in front of his/her eyes. And in such a situation, these rascals can think of nothing but profits!!

- Most people value the acquisitions defined by macroeconomics and this is a narrow notion.

- I had never realized that every day he noticed me walking past him during my evening walk; it started with a hand wave and then an exchange of friendly words. He also knew where I lived. Today he stood in front of his luxurious house watering his plants and I stopped by. I said, "Nice house uncle!" He said, "I had to struggle a lot to build this house and now I realize, that this is too big for me and my family. Yours is an apt one." It felt as if he was a little aggrieved. Nevertheless, I thanked him for his words.

- 7 basic needs of a human must be fulfilled before he starts enquiring about his being before he tries to enlighten his consciousness before he treads the path of spirituality.

- British owe reparations, to the Indian government. And for full 190 years, 1 month and 23 days not only since the Queens proclamation 1858.

- There is a lot of mess going on in African nations that go unreported in our newspapers. That's the result of drawing horizontal and vertical lines on a map, in a diplomatic room of Berlin.

- The cold war era taught us one thing, that psycho politicians are a real threat to humanity.

- Are you amazed by the military strength of Israel!! (a nation which is not even visible on the world map) Well, don't be! That is what a human or a group of humans can do when their existence is under threat.

- They have ranked Ranjit Singh as the greatest ruler of the 19th century. He truly deserves that. During his 38 year rule, he checked the Afghans in the west, British in the east and captured Aksai Chin in the North (which now lies with China). From Khyber to Sutlej he had built a vast empire. But there was one issue that he was a "state in person", maybe that's why Punjab succumbed to the British within 10 years of his death. Anyhow, his commander Hari Singh Nalwa also deserves a rank in the list of top 10 army generals, of the 19th century.

- Freedom can be claimed at any moment in your life. All you need to do is first realize that you don't have it and secondly overcome the fear of asking for it.

- Only a person who lacks insecurities can tread on difficult paths of life. People who are scared often don't take the risk.

- I look back and it's damn 7 years of struggle. How did I make it up till here?

- In the last decade, my mind has often confronted my heart. No doubt, my heart has often won, but every time, it has pained me a lot.

- Shawshank redemption, probably the greatest film of all times, flopped in the cinema halls in 1994. Now IMDB rates it 9.3. The value of great things is understood quite slowly and gradually.

A Word To The Readers

It is impossible to write 40,000 words without mistakes. Therefore I request my readers to please communicate me the mistakes, if any, on the email : aclimbthroughthemist@gmail.com. I will also appreciate your worthy feedback, not only via this email but also, on all the platforms where this book is available. Wishing the best for you. Thanks a lot!

-Jashandeep Singh Kang